I love the notion of "storm sisters"—soul friends who help us get through life's most raw and painful transitions. In her new book, Afton Rorvik invites readers to "reach for friendship" when we struggle. Part memoir and part spiritual guide, *Storm Sisters* is an excellent resource for women's groups and retreats. Read it with the women who show up for you and find new, life-giving ways to support your spiritual sisters when they are navigating hard times."

Jennifer Grant, Author of *Love You More, MOMumental, Wholehearted Living,* and *Disquiet Time*

Storm Sisters is an authentic and encouraging book in which the author shares how to walk through both the highs and lows of life with a friend. Yet this book is more than a how-to manual. Each chapter will invite the reader to engage in self-reflection through suggested journal questions. *Storm Sisters* is a must-read for the mind, emotions, and the soul."

Jennifer Stenzel, Licensed Clinical Professional Counselor and Executive Director of Stenzel Clinical Services, Ltd.

As Afton travels through the storm of losing her mother, the Bible is her boat. Through the rough currents of life, she shares how she has drawn strength from that source . . . She encourages you to search out and enrich your life with the sisterhood relationships that help stay your course. Very well written and touches your heart.

Karolyn Grimes, Zuzu Bailey in the holiday film *It's a Wonderful Life*

Tears streamed down my cheeks as I read *Storm Sisters* and was reminded of precious friends who have been present in my own painful struggles. Afton Rorvik's stories of the blessing of friends who walk beside us during struggles are a precious reminder that God calls us to be encouragement, strength and help for one another. Afton's gentle stories of her own difficult times and those of her friends are wonderful reminders of the blessing of friends who show up to do those things as they gently point us to God's presence and love . . . even when life is very painful.

Carolyn Larsen, author of the best-selling
The Little Girls Bible Storybook for Mothers and Daughters

Deep female friendships do not come naturally to all women. Personally, I have often admired them from afar, but not known how to engage in them in my own life. Author Afton Rorvik models these friendships in her book *Storm Sisters*. As I read, I implemented her ideas, contacting friends who are enduring storms. Afton gave beautiful words to my heartfelt emotions, borrowing them from her book made caring for my friends more doable.

Marie Allison, Director Connect Ministry, Wheaton Bible Church

We've all been through the storms of life. What a comfort to know the One who quiets the winds and calms the raging seas—and sometimes uses our sisters-in-Christ to do it. In *Storm Sisters*, Afton Rorvik shares the wisdom she gained on her journey through a difficult storm, and introduces us to the godly women who supported her along the way. Full of depth and biblical comfort, this book is a must-read for all women. Because at some time or other we will all need, or need to be, a "storm sister."

Virginia Smith, bestselling author of the *Sister-to-Sister Series*
and *Rainy Day Dreams*

Afton has written a transparent and open account of struggle and loss, and what it means to have your sisters of the heart walk with you along life's challenging paths. Readers will find themselves inspired, and they will also discover thought-provoking questions to help them explore their own hopes, needs and directions. Thus, *Storm Sisters* becomes a dialogue, an encouragement and a help in difficult times.

Liz Duckworth, author of *A Perfect Word for Every Occasion*
and *Wildflower Living*

STORM
SISTERS

STORM
SISTERS

FRIENDS THROUGH
ALL SEASONS

AFTON RORVIK

WORTHY
Inspired

For John, my "beste venn"
and storm-strong husband

"A new command I give you: Love one another.
As I have loved you, so you must love one another.
By this everyone will know that you are my disciples,
if you love one another."

—

John 13:34-35, NIV

Table of Contents

Foreword

by Mary Whelchel

We often say, "Well, that's just life," but when we are personally in the midst of "life"—one of those inevitable storms—
the clichés don't help. Even the well-intended reminders that
"all things work together for our good" can fall on resentful
ears and cause us to curl up and isolate.

Getting through life's storms for those of us who are
Christ-followers is uniquely challenging. After all, we're sup-
posed to have all the answers. Somehow—somewhere—we
sisters have gotten this erroneous idea that being strong
means never admitting we can't make it on our own. Yet the
Bible shows us a different picture.

I think of Mary traveling to see her cousin, Elizabeth, as
soon as the angel announced that she would give birth to the
Messiah. She needed a sister who understood what she was
facing; she needed someone to simply listen and encourage
and be there for her as she processed this life-changing event
coming her way. As was prophesied, though she was the most

blessed woman who ever lived, a sword would pierce her soul, and there were many storms ahead for her. She needed Elizabeth.

In a truly transparent and genuine way, Afton shows us how the sisterhood of believers is intended to work. Through her own storms and those of her friends, she beautifully illustrates the basic principles we need to know in order to help each other navigate our storms. She gives us a clear picture of what it means to weep with those who weep.

I've known Afton since before she married my good friend, John, and I've watched her walk through these storms. I've seen how she has learned to share her struggles, her doubts, her fears with her sisters, and how she has been there for them when they couldn't see through their own clouds of doubt and fear. As a leader of women in my church, I see again and again how desperately we need each other. God never intended for us to walk through our storms alone.

This book will give you hope in your storm. It will give you guidance and ideas on how to reach out to your sisters in their storms. It will take you deeper into the Bible to fortify your soul, and you will be better prepared to be a storm sister.

Acknowledgments

I am grateful to so many people who helped this book come to life:

— My mother, who although she claimed the title of introvert, showed me the value of connection to other women and the strength that comes from loving God.

— My mother's friends who gave so much of themselves to her and to me in her last few months on this earth. If only I had space to tell all of your kindnesses.

— My brothers, who have shared so many life storms with me.

— My sisters-in-law and mother-in-law, who have become family as well as friends.

— My childhood friends, Kim, Roberta, and Ann who grew up with me in life and in faith.

— Karen and Karyn, who have read so much of my writing for so long and never failed to speak God's truth and grace to me.

— My BCM girls from college days, who continually show me the light of God and challenge me to keep my eyes heavenward.

— My neighbors, Bev and Julie, who share life with me, including dog walks and coffee moments, and do not fear to walk with me in storms.

— My Thursday morning Bible study group, who prayed me through this journey to publication.

— My dear friend and mentor, Helen deVette, who pushed and challenged me, all with an enormous dose of encouragement. "Thanks be to God!"

— My agent, Dan Balow, who believed in me and pushed me to pursue this dream.

— My editor, Christina Honea, at Worthy Publishing and the entire team at Worthy, especially Troy Johnson, Mark Gilroy, and Bart Dawson, who shared and enhanced my vision for this book.

— My children, Karl and Annalisa, who have taught me so much about myself and helped me to be "real."

— My storm-strong husband, John, who makes me laugh, helps me keep life in perspective, and joins me in pounding the gates of heaven in prayer.

Introduction

Storm Sister (n) – a friend who sticks close when storms hit her friend's life. Such a friend might also go by the title of sister, longtime friend, rediscovered friend, or acquaintance who offers or accepts friendship in a crisis. *This type of friendship particularly thrives among women connected first to God.*

As I faced some rough, seemingly unrelenting storms in my life, I struggled to stand and not lose myself or my faith. In the midst of it all, I discovered that I had friends who willingly offered to walk with me through my dark days—Storm Sisters.

In the pages that follow, I want to introduce you to some of these remarkable women and gift you with the wisdom they gave me. I want you to know Michelle and Roberta, my stalwart Storm Sisters and longtime friends. And I want you to meet my mother's wise friends, whom I did not really know until my mother became ill.

You don't have to claim the title of extrovert to become a Storm Sister. I know. I am a certified introvert, steeped in Lone-Ranger tendencies. And yet, God has opened my eyes to this marvelous gift of connectedness with other women, a gift I don't want you to miss.

Let this book help you unwrap this gift from God, this gift of connectedness:

> *But our bodies have many parts, and God has put each part just where he wants it. How strange a body would be if it had only one part! Yes, there are many parts, but only one body. The eye can never say to the hand, "I don't need you." The head can't say to the feet, "I don't need you. . . . " All of you together are Christ's body, and each of you is a part of it* (1 Corinthians 12:18-21, 27, NLT).

Come with me on this journey. And don't miss the opportunity to start your own journey as a Storm Sister by using the study guide for each chapter at the end of the book.

Chapter 1

Ingredients for
Everyday Friendship

Friendship. Not a word I really understood or experienced until my teen years.

Growing up on two acres in rural Colorado, I spent my free time wandering through the tall grass on our property or lying on my back in a hammock in the summer and devouring books. Sometimes I tried to speak "sheep" to our ever-tolerant neighbors to the east. I even serenaded them on occasion with my clarinet.

My father, a modern-day Thoreau and also an alcoholic, chose isolation over community living. His choices, by default, became my choices. On the bus ride home every day from elementary school, I would look at the neighborhoods we passed—houses close together without barbed-wire fences to separate them. *What would it feel like,* I wondered, *to live so close to people?*

And then I became a teenager and entered junior high. Girls started going shopping together. They invited me—quiet, shy, sheep-talking me! I scrambled to learn how to make friends. What should I say? What should I wear? What mattered to them? What mattered to me?

Friendship 101 . . . and Faith

As I jumped into Friendship 101, I also jumped into Faith 101.

In my early teens I made a decision to give all of myself to God and try to live for Him. So, for me, the discovery of friendship and faith became intertwined. As I began testing the friendship waters, I also began studying the Bible with other girls and an adult leader from our youth group. Once a week, every week, we met together.

A girl in the lunch line might have made fun of me that morning for my rather pointy ears; my father might have erupted in a rage at a song I started singing that afternoon; my mouth might ache from my recently tightened braces.

But on this night, with these people, I could forget the hard parts of life. I could enjoy connection—belonging.

These people expected me. Every week after our lesson from the Bible, we would spend some time praying. I sat and listened to our leader and these other girls talk to God as if He knew them and cared about the details of their lives. *Could God care about me—quiet, shy, sheep-loving me?!*

I wanted to know more about this God.

Because getting out of a warm bed in the morning challenged me, I set my clock radio to the local hog reports every morning at 6:30. Nothing like hearing a voice spew out the prices of hogs to motivate me to jump out of bed!

And perhaps because my mother loved the Psalms and talked about them, I began to read them for myself in those early morning hours. Again, I discovered honest conversation with God. David talked to God about his enemies, his fears, his failures, his future. . . . I found myself borrowing David's words and using them to talk to God about my own enemies, fears, failures, future. . . .

> *But thou, O LORD, art a shield for me; my glory, and the lifter up of mine head. I cried unto the Lord with my voice, and he heard me out of his holy hill. Selah.*

*I laid me down and slept; I awaked; for the Lord
sustained me* (Psalm 3:3-5, KJV).

In those early mornings, I forged a relationship with
God—a friendship.

Much to my surprise, my friendship with God gave me
courage to connect to other people. As I began to understand
His great love for me, I grew in my courage and confidence to
face the confusing, crowded worlds of junior high and high
school.

I knew that no matter what happened during the day—
whether I said the wrong thing, or didn't say anything when I
so desperately wanted to, or if I wore something horribly out-
of-fashion that drew attention to my homemade clothes—
God cared.

As I continued to study the Bible with girls my age, we
talked over how to live out what we studied. What does it
mean to "love one another" as mentioned in 1 John 3:11?
What does "bearing one another's burdens" (Galatians 6:2)
look like in real life? When Romans 12:15 calls us to "weep
with those who weep," how do we sincerely accomplish
that?

In college I continued to connect with women who asked these same kinds of questions. Living together in close quarters brought to life all of our quirky habits—singing in the shower at 5 a.m., writing papers in the closet late at night while eating crackers—but because of our shared faith and commitment to connectedness as ordained by God, we stuck with each other. We made time for meals together; we stayed up late and made popcorn and talked. We challenged each other to know God and ourselves better.

Have you experienced the joy of connectedness—God's gift? If not, what one tiny step could you take today in that direction?

I did not know then that these habits of connectedness would mean that these women— all of them—would remain my close friends many decades later. We continue to make time for each other, now in regular emails. We continue to challenge each other to think about God and ourselves. We continue to go the extra mile for each other and our families. We travel to each other's homes.

Storm Sisters all.

We did not set out to become Storm Sisters; we set out to live as God called us to live: connected.

Every Week . . .

Just as I met with a group of girls every week in junior high and on into high school, I now meet with my husband every week.

Over the past twenty-seven years, my husband and I have come to use the term *beste venn* for each other. In Norwegian it means "best friend." Although the phrase rolls off our lips these days, the making of this friendship took, and still takes, great intent.

And lunch every Friday.

We created "Friday Lunch" eighteen years ago, the year our youngest child went to first grade. Since that day we have fought fiercely to keep this weekly date by saying no to other lunch invitations, rescheduling meetings. . . . Our friends, children, employers, and neighbors know, "Don't mess with Friday Lunch!"

Even on the days when we feel out of sorts with each other for one reason or another, we keep our Friday lunch. And we continually save coupons for local restaurants.

Every week.

The keeping of this date reminds us both that we belong to each other. That someone cares. It seems that God continually reinforces to me that lesson He began to teach me in junior high.

As John and I have grown in our love for God and for each other, we have also intentionally tried to build other friendships. He has a shortlist of men he regularly calls and emails and goes to see. I have a similar shortlist of women I see consistently and others I email with every week. I have to keep the list short. As my children tell me, I'm not good at multi-tasking. I just can't juggle 374 friends. Not in a way that makes them feel I truly care.

Time. Intention. Care.

All prompted by the example of the great love God has lavished on us: "No one has ever seen God. But if we love each other, God lives in us, and his love is brought to full expression in us" (1 John 4:12, NLT).

Choosing People

I now live in an "I'll-keep-your-dog-while-you're-out-of-town" sort of neighborhood. Much of that happened because the extroverts in our midst love to get together. But some of it happened because of something a small group of us—

women—did together for almost seven years.

Every other Thursday, we met together. And then some years it became every other Tuesday or the first Monday of the month.

We spent time talking about our latest house projects, who was moving in or out, the upcoming fun fair at the local elementary school. . . . We drank decaf together, some flavored, some straight black.

And we studied the Bible.

Some of us had grown up reading the Bible; some of us had just discovered it; some of us had never read it. We jumped into reading and talking about the Gospel of Mark.

As the weeks went on, we worked hard to listen to each other, encouraging exploration and questions. Who were these Pharisees? Why did they have such a strong negative opinion of Jesus? Why did Jesus teach with parables? Really? Couldn't He just have told it like it was? What did Jesus mean when He said, "Let the little children come to me, and do not hinder them, for the kingdom of God belongs to such as these" (Mark 10:14, NIV)?

After we studied Mark, we moved on to other books in the Bible. We talked, we laughed, we learned to pray for each other. And we became friends.

Although we don't officially meet these days, some of us still gather our families together for shared dinners. For six years running, four or five of these women with their husbands arrange childcare and take vacation days to spend a long weekend together in Door County.

I now live in a neighborhood without barbed-wire fences or sheep, and I live within the community of believers, the church. I'm not budging. I need only open my front door and walk steps to the door of a Storm Sister. Every day I thank God for that gift.

No more conversations with sheep. I will reach for people, God's creation. As you begin this book, I pray that you, too, will make a decision to reach for people—for friendship. May you come to know, as I have, this rich, blessed gift from God.

What If?

How amazing that this book, the Bible, can so shape us, teaching us to know God and to know each other. What might happen in your life, in your relationships, if you let God and the Bible take center stage?

Chapter 2

When the Storms Come

Michelle and I have called each other "friend" for decades. At this age, we're not counting exactly how many decades. We met our freshman year of college and then shared our first apartment together after college. She introduced me to gourmet coffee, and I introduced her to Shakespeare. We made runs for deep-dish pizza together. I still have the dress I wore in Michelle's wedding. My daughter latched onto it as a child and dubbed it her favorite princess dress-up dress—one she wouldn't share. I have apologized many times to Michelle for the pink, puffy-sleeved dress she had to wear in my wedding.

In 2005, long after those college days and our weddings, storms invaded Michelle's life, followed shortly by storms in my own life. Not just heavy spring cloudbursts but hurricane-strength storms that took our breath away and made us both want to run for cover.

Our phone conversations and coffee runs no longer focused on kids and swimming lessons, household projects, or upcoming vacations. Instead we discussed such topics as chemotherapy and a rare neurological disease with a hard-to-pronounce German name. The pain felt so real and so deep.

At some point one of us stumbled upon a verse in a little-known book of the Old Testament:

> *I remember my affliction and my wandering, the bitterness and the gall. I well remember them, and my soul is downcast within me. Yet this I call to mind and therefore I have hope: Because of the LORD's great love we are not consumed, for his compassions never fail. They are new every morning; great is your faithfulness* (Lamentations 3:19-23, NIV).

This became our shared mantra: "Because of the LORD's great love, we are not consumed." Sometimes we simply ended a phone conversation or quick cup of coffee with, "We are not consumed."

Bracing for the Incoming Storm

Just after Thanksgiving dinner 2005, my phone rang. On the other end my youngest brother, Joe, explained, "Mom came to see us for Thanksgiving and just doesn't seem right. She has trouble seeing, and her balance is off. She doesn't remember some things. We have taken her to the hospital. We don't know what is wrong."

I gasped. I had just seen my mother a month before. She seemed as independent and strong as always. Had she experienced *a stroke?*

After many more tests and the careful consultation of a well-regarded neurologist, the results pointed to a rare neurological disease: Creutzfeldt-Jakob disease (CJD). This rare, degenerative,

Do you have a friend in a storm? Consider finding a passage in the Bible to send her in an email or card. Then write that same passage down and put it where you will see it and commit to pray those words over your friend each day.

invariably fatal brain disorder affects about one in one million people per year worldwide, usually appears in later life, and runs a rapid course. Those cold, hard facts from The National Institute of Neurological Disorders and Stroke gave me a sick sense of foreboding. *What lay ahead? Could I handle it?*

As I prepared to go see my brother and sort through with him what we should do next for our mother, I told a few close friends and asked them to pray. One friend of many years, Karyn, responded simply by emailing me these words from Psalm 121 (NASB):

> *I will lift up my eyes to the mountains;*
> *From whence shall my help come?*
> *My help comes from the Lord,*
> *Who made heaven and earth . . .*
> *He who keeps you will not slumber . . .*
> *The Lord is your keeper;*
> *The Lord is your shade on your right hand . . .*
> *The Lord will guard your going out and your coming in*
> *From this time forth and forever.*

Karyn relied on timeless, true words, words that never fail—God's words. And I would need them too.

Hanging on to Storm-Strong Words

When I arrived in Albany, Mom did not want to discuss her diagnosis. She wanted to go home. I quickly discovered that if she overheard me talking about her on the phone, she would become angry. When I managed a quick phone call to my husband, I could not let my anxiety and fear for my mom spill out, even as sobs filled my heart. And, unless I ducked out of the apartment in freezing-winter weather, I could not verbally explain to our two children (12 and 16) that their Nana was dying.

Joe and I began to make plans for getting Mom home and then finding good care for her. But we had to do it largely without talking out loud. We developed a system of emailing each other across his living room. How life-giving those words became as they reminded me that I did not face this mighty storm alone.

During those silent days, many other family members and friends emailed and voiced their support. One of these friends, Mary, wrote:

I know you're missing your family back here now, but John declares they're doing okay. Don't forget this wonderful passage from Isaiah 43:1-3 (NIV):

But now, this is what the Lord says—he who created you, Jacob, he who formed you, Israel: "Do not fear, for I have redeemed you; I have summoned you by name; you are mine. When you pass through the waters, I will be with you; and when you pass through the rivers, they will not sweep over you. When you walk through the fire, you will not be burned; the flames will not set you ablaze. For I am the Lord your God, the Holy One of Israel, your Savior."

You're passing through deep waters, but you're never alone.

Longing to Run Away

One afternoon, Joe stepped out to run a few errands and catch his breath. By now he had stopped attending his graduate courses in architecture. His patient, thoughtful wife who worked with brain-injured patients had left for work many hours ago. Mom and I were alone in the apartment.

While I responded to emails, Mom crossed the room and stood next to me.

"Did you tell people about my CJD?"

I nodded. "I did. I'm sorry. I feel sad about all of this. I needed to tell people and have them pray for me. I need help with this."

"Well, I can't help you," she stated loudly. "Call John! Call John! I can't help you!"

By now my sobs came full-force. That made Mom even more angry. I escaped to a room in the apartment and locked the door,

We all fear saying the wrong thing. If you can't trust your own words, know that you can surely trust God's words in the Bible.

listening to Mom's continued shouting, and dialed my husband. I whispered into the cell phone what had just happened.

I told him that I really wanted just to get on an airplane and go home.

Later that night, my cell phone rang. I ran to a quiet corner of the apartment and answered it. My mother-in-law's kind voice said, "John called us and told us that things are hard for you out there. I know you can't talk much. Just know that Poppo (my father-in-law) and I love you and that you are doing the right thing. You are where you need to be."

Those words settled into my heart and gave me courage and perspective. Later that night, these words from the Psalms also gave me courage and perspective: "The LORD is my light and my salvation—whom shall I fear? The LORD is the stronghold of my life—of whom shall I be afraid? . . . Though an army besiege me, my heart will not fear; though war break out against me, even then will I be confident" (Psalm 27:1-2, NIV).

Choosing to Stay

The next morning, I rolled up my sleeves, prayed for strength, and resolved to stay. As Mom began to anticipate going home, she talked often of her "700 friends." She confidently explained that these friends, most of them women, would surround her and help her. I grinned and nodded my head, thinking that Mom certainly exaggerated in both the number of friends she had and also in her adamant conviction of their eagerness to help her.

And then I began to get emails from some of these "700 friends," some of whom I knew, but many I did not know.

Afton, I am depending on you and Joe to be honest with me about how I can help. . . . You know, nothing is hard for me to see. One of the joys of being a nurse throughout my life is that I now am at ease with almost anything that human life offers in the way of behavior and need. So, I will not be troubled if your mom cannot be herself with me. I love her, as you do (well, not as deeply as you, of course), and want to do what is helpful. I also do not want to be in the way. So, I need you to be open with me about what can be helpful.

I check my email in the morning about 7 a.m., and then again usually at about noon, and then again at about supper time. So, if it is easier to communicate by email then I will be diligent in getting back to you quickly.

Love to you all,

Judy L.

Soon, I began to see with my own eyes what Mom meant. I also began to catch my first glimpse of Storm Sisterhood as described in Proverbs 17:17: "A friend loves at all times, and a brother is born for adversity" (NIV). What a gift I received from these "700 friends" of my mother's, well-practiced in the art of Storm Sisterhood.

What If?

When storms come, we naturally want to run. What might happen in your friendships if you learned instead to stay put when storms hit?

Chapter 3

Asking for Help

Dear Friends—

I'm sending this email to you to ask you to pray for our family. We have recently discovered that my mom has Creutzfeldt-Jakob Disease.

At the moment she is in New York with my youngest brother. On Tuesday I will join them in New York. Then on Saturday I will take my mom home.

Please pray that we will have wisdom to do the most helpful, kind thing for my mom. Also please pray that I will make good connections with people who can help in Colorado. Through it all, please pray that we do not lose sight of heaven.

This is all a great challenge on many fronts.

Blessings, Afton Rorvik

This email became my first cry for help, my first admission that I needed and wanted companions on this as-yet-unknown journey. But even as I sent out that email, I questioned myself. *Had I asked too much from friends to enter with me into this horrific situation?* I have never asked for help well. I am much more comfortable helping than receiving help.

Where do you fall on the spectrum of letting friends help you? Do you struggle with admitting your need? What keeps you from saying something? Take a moment now and ask God to help you embrace your weakness so that He can show Himself strong in it.

Why do I think I have to keep my weaknesses to myself? Perhaps it comes down to thinking that I will honor God more by talking about His good work in my life rather than what I struggle to understand. Yet, throughout the Bible, I read about many imperfect men and women.

When the Apostle Paul wrote about his weakness, he concluded, "For when I am weak, than I am strong" (2 Corinthians 12:10, NIV). What a paradox. Paul, a well-educated, godly man, seemed to have a direct line to God. And yet he also had a personal weakness, something he called a "thorn in the flesh." Whatever it was, Paul did not try to pretend it away. He openly acknowledged it.

My "Help!" email generated a lot of responses, including one from a friend, Roberta, whom I met in English class during our first year of junior high. During our teenage years I spent a lot of time at her house and even more time on the phone talking to her. (I still have her phone number memorized!) Although neither one of us settled in our hometown, we somehow managed to stay in touch over many decades, largely due to Roberta's regular, newsy, and thoughtful letters.

Hi Afton,

I'm sure it helps to see your mom in person and to be able to give her a hug and see with your own eyes how she is feeling. Please give her an extra hug from me, too. You might tell her that I was thinking of her so much last Friday when I was sitting next to a karate mom that knit just the way your mom taught me.

I know that your family misses you, but that you need to be right where you are right now.

You are all in our prayers. Keep on keeping on. . . .

Love, Berta

Back in the days of acne and braces, I had no idea that I would make a lifetime friend. Roberta, who long ago listened to me go on and on about boys, now willingly listened to me as I wrote and talked on the phone about the pain of watching my mother suffer. Roberta had watched her own father die from cancer a few years earlier. She knew so well the ache of watching a parent decline.

What strength friendship provides.

Wise King Solomon knew this: "Two people are better off than one, for they can help each other succeed. If one person falls, the other can reach out and help. But someone who falls alone is in real trouble" (Ecclesiastes 4:9-10, NLT).

"Do It, Self!"

In early December we settled Mom in her own house, surrounded by her books. I can only imagine how agonizing it must have been for her to look at her bookcases—one in every room, including the garage—and know that she could not read any of them. As long as I can remember, my mother read books while knitting at the same time. She tackled medieval literature in German, knitting patterns in Norwegian, theology, bestsellers. . . .

Now she faced long, empty days with a brain that just wouldn't do what she continually prodded it to do.

I watched as she visited with some of her "700 friends" who stopped by. She put on a big smile, picked up her knitting, and settled into her favorite chair. She willed herself to focus and carry on a conversation. When each guest left, she settled into a silent exhaustion.

Giving in or giving up didn't figure into Mom's vocabulary—ever. Throughout her life she pushed herself to do what needed doing, even if that meant constructing a wooden, backyard fence by herself. Now she remained adamant that she could stay in her own house, reminding me of my two-year-old son who announced frequently: "Do it, self!"

Like my mother, I skew toward "doing it self." Paul's words challenge me:

> But our bodies have many parts, and God has put each part just where he wants it. How strange a body would be if it had only one part! Yes, there are many parts, but only one body. The eye can never say to the hand, "I don't need you." The head can't say to

*the feet, "I don't need you. . . ." All of you togeth-
er are Christ's body, and each of you is a part of it*
(1 Corinthians 12:18-21, 27, NLT).

Join me in praying that we would recognize when our
"Do it self" attitude keeps us from growing into women who
know how to connect.

Being First to Say, "Help Me, Please"

Being first to ask for help in a friendship takes courage . . .
and humility.

Months before my mom's issues developed, Michelle
and I caught up on the phone. Nothing much new. But, Megan (age three) had an appointment scheduled with an ENT
for an ear infection that just wouldn't go away.

That appointment launched Michelle on a journey she
could never have imagined. A journey that included hospital
visits and chemotherapy for a rare childhood disease. And a
journey that included asking friends for help.

"Can you pick up Calvin (age five) from his summer
class and then give him dinner and put him to bed? That way

Ryan can be here with me at the hospital."

"Yes!"

Later, when I learned about my mom's situation, I remembered Michelle's "help" phone call. Because she had let me into the stormy place in her life, I knew that I could do the same.

Although Michelle preferred to talk on the phone, she learned to email so that we could stay in touch during my storm. She told me about the ups and downs of Megan's treatments, and I told her about the ups and downs of trying to help my mom.

> *Ryan and I read Psalm 139 out loud to each other last night, after you had said it was helpful to you. What a comfort! So many of the Psalms have helped me over the past few months—ones that are so familiar but meet the new situation head-on. Psalm 42 has meant so much to me lately.*

Michelle could have chosen to keep her struggles to herself, but because she did not, I experienced both the joy of providing comfort and receiving comfort.

Paul said it so eloquently: "Praise be to the God and

Father of our Lord Jesus Christ, the Father of compassion and the God of all comfort, who comforts us in all our troubles, so that we can comfort those in any trouble with the comfort we ourselves receive from God" (2 Corinthians 1:3-4, NIV).

"Thank You for Helping"

For most of December 2005 I traveled back and forth between Illinois and Colorado.

By late December, Mom had declined so much that I worried about just keeping her safe in her own house. Mom did not see it that way. She remained convinced that she could will herself to push through any situation.

One night Joe, my younger brother, and I sat together and tried to talk quietly in Mom's basement after we knew she was in bed. "I am so afraid Mom will hurt herself. We can't stay with her all the time, but she doesn't want a caregiver to move in with her. What can we do?"

At that moment the phone rang. Joe jumped to grab it quickly before Mom became agitated trying to answer it. On the other end Mom's best friend, Judy M., asked about our situation. She quickly heard the desperation and sadness in Joe's voice. Shortly after that conversation Judy sent out an email asking for people to help.

As I watched the network of Mom's friends form and surround her with short visits, love, and prayers, I marveled. This was the crazy month of December and these women had families of their own. Some, like Judy, also juggled full-time jobs. Still, they came. And, much to my surprise, they surrounded me.

Please know that we love you, as well as your Mom. It is a truth that sometimes the whole experience is harder on those who are family than on the person experiencing the decline. So be good to yourself, and ask us for what you need when you are not here.

What If?

We all struggle to recognize and admit our need. What might happen if in just one friendship, you both found the courage to speak of your deep-down needs?

Chapter 4

Resisting the Urge
to Fix

To-do lists. Projects with deadlines and measurable results. They make me happy. I can see what I should do and when I should do it. I can roll up my sleeves and "just get it done."

When I put my list-making self on the plane to go help my mom, I, of course, went with a list of questions. Practical questions:

- If you need 24/7 care, where do you want to be?
- In the event you become unable to pay bills, who do you want to handle your finances?
- Do you want to give us your email password?

I knew that Mom had a terminal illness and that I could not cure her. But I did so want to use my strength, brain, and will to tidy up this messy situation.

One night after sitting at dinner and watching Mom struggle to place her glass back on the table after taking a sip, I decided to ask one of my questions.

"Mom, how will you get food for yourself when you get home?" She lived alone. The nearest grocery store was at least a mile away. I feared that she would try to drive her car even though the glass-at-the-table incident showed me that her eyesight had become unreliable.

I wanted to get this figured out, start arranging things. . . . Mom did not. I pushed. She pushed back.

I had asked a reasonable question. A practical one. But losing yourself in pieces—eyesight, balance, great intelligence, dignity—defies practical answers.

The Bible has wise words to say about keeping to-dos in perspective: "Now listen, you who say, 'Today or tomorrow we will go to this or that city, spend a year there, carry on business and make money.' Why, you do not even know what will happen tomorrow. What is your life? You are a mist that appears for a little while and then vanishes" (James 4:13-14, NIV).

Listening, Not Fixing

As the day loomed closer for our trip to take Mom home, my list of questions remained unanswered. What would we do? How could we keep Mom safe? How could she live alone in her own house once we had to leave?

One weekend afternoon while Joe and I stepped out to run an errand and catch our breath, my sister-in-law, Sarjan, sat down and had a conversation with Mom.

When we returned, Sarjan quietly showed us a list of things she and Mom had talked about. Mom had agreed not to get groceries by herself. We could ask a designated friend to help with that. She also said that another friend could help her pay her bills, etc. She wanted to do her own laundry. . . .

What happened? How did Sarjan get to this point with Mom?

Over the months that followed I began to see what a gift Sarjan had for affirming Mom's dignity and strength while also talking with her about challenges she faced. She would say things like, "I know how much you like singing in

How do you balance the daily to-do list and the desire to jump in and tidy situations with the long-term awareness of the shortness of life?

choir at your church. Let's talk about how we can help you do that on Christmas Eve."

I imagine that her conversation with Mom that afternoon included questions like: "How are you feeling about going home? What are you looking forward to? What are you worried about? How might some of us help you?"

Practical questions mattered, yes, but Sarjan knew what mattered most—Mom.

In Philippians 2, the Apostle Paul writes about the tender way God treated us and encourages us to treat each other with this same love. Later in the chapter he also writes about his partner in ministry, Timothy: "I have no one else like him, who takes a genuine interest in your welfare" (Philippians 2:20, NIV).

Pointing, Not Fixing

Many months before I learned of my mom's condition, while Michelle and her husband met with doctors about their daughter's condition, I hung out with five-year-old Calvin for most of two days. We played with his magnetic link set and read stories. He explained his latest elaborate cardboard building projects to me. He helped me do laundry at my house and beat me in multiple games of foosball. After dinner at our house that second night, I drove Calvin home to put him to bed.

"When will Daddy be home? Will you be here in the morning? Is Megan still in the hospital? Will Mom be home tomorrow?"

I wanted to give Calvin concrete answers for all his questions. A firm yes or firm no. A specific time frame. I wanted to make everything feel better for him. And I wanted to make everything better for my friend. If I could just make all of this go away. . . .

"Hey, Calvin. Let's play a game. See these cards? Let's draw an arrow on every card. Then after you go to bed, I'll put the cards on the floor outside your room. Either the cards will point toward your parents' room because one of them is home, or they will point to your living room where I will be sleeping on your sofa. Either way, just follow the arrows, you will find a person."

My arrow-game didn't bring instant healing to my friend's daughter. It didn't give Calvin the answers he so longed for. It did, however, remind him that he was not alone. A person who loved him waited at the end of the arrow-path.

Don't we all need such a reminder in the middle of a storm?

> *O Lord, you have examined my heart and know*
> *everything about me. . . . You go before me and follow*
> *me. You place your hand of blessing on my head*
> (Psalm 139:1, 5, NLT).

Supporting, Not Fixing

Making everything better, keeping people happy. . . . Although I never write these words on my to-do lists, I should because they figure prominently in everything I do. Especially when someone I love, like my mom, hurts.

I knew Peggy, or rather I knew her one-of-a-kind handmade quilts. Beautiful. Detailed. One of Mom's "700 friends," she had heard about Mom's illness and emailed me: "I am in shock and ever so sorry. . . . What can I do to help? Know that I care and am thinking of all of you and that I am SO, SO sorry."

Many years earlier, when I was about eight months pregnant with our son, Mom suddenly discovered that she needed major surgery. I couldn't come. Mom couldn't travel. She lived alone but needed someone with her after surgery.

Peggy stepped in, welcoming Mom into her home while she convalesced.

Now, more than fifteen years later, Mom insisted that Peggy not help her or visit her. I don't know why. Mom probably didn't even know why. One of the symptoms of her illness, which now controlled her brain, was that she began to push certain people away. People she had known well. People who had loved her well.

I felt I had to honor my mom's request even though I did not understand it. And so I called Peggy. She responded simply: "I understand, and I will honor your mom's request even though I would love to see her. Why don't you come over next week for a cup of tea?"

A cup of tea? Really? How could she respond with such kindness and grace?

That cup of tea led to another and another. We talked about the woman my mother had been, including the way she would show up to visit with flowers from her garden. We also talked about the death of Peggy's first husband and how her friends stood with her when she could hardly stand herself. Not once did she speak ill of Mom or demand to see her. Instead, she gently helped me embrace the process of death and grief.

Mercy. Even more beautiful than handmade quilts.

How easily Peggy, or any one of my mother's "700 friends" could have said to us, "I know what would be best for your mom. . . ."

They had lived longer than my brothers and I had. And had more experience with death. They knew our mother in ways that we did not. Several of them had medical backgrounds.

At any point, they could have swept into her house and into our lives and said, "We'll tell you what to do." Instead, they went to see Mom and listened to her and cried with her. After the visits, they often sent emails about their visit that included observations about Mom's concerns and declining abilities. They became our eyes and ears when we could not sit at Mom's side. But they did far more than that.

> *Your mother talks of needing time alone, but when alone, she has difficulty. And,*
>
> > *I have observed how she can control her conversations to sound very much in charge and capable, but then is not really being able to truly do basic tasks.*

My heart aches for you as you try to make good decisions. . . . We all wish we could find the right answers for your mother's care but know there is no 'right' only your best judgment—and we will help by supporting whatever that judgment is.

Supporting . . . not fixing.

The Bible tells the story of Job, a man who suffered many storms and great loss, including the lives of many family members. His friends Eliphaz, Bildad, Zophar, and Elihu all tried to comfort him. At one point the youngest of the group, Elihu, says: "Pay attention, Job, and listen to me; be silent, and I will speak" (Job 33:31, NIV).

Ouch! Seems Elihu wanted to fix . . . like me.

What If?

We all have so much to do every day and so many people who depend on us to help them. What would happen to our daily to-do list if we first wrote at the top of it, "Don't fix"?

Chapter 5

Weeping with Those Who Weep

"Hi, Aftonian. I don't have much time, but I wanted you to know that the doctor found a mass behind Megan's ear."

"Oh, Michelle!" I could feel the tears starting to come and my voice starting to waver. I fought them back. "I'll pray. Keep me posted."

As soon as I hung up the phone, I burst into tears. *How could this happen to sweet little Megan?* Memories of my own daughter at age three filled my head. Three-year-olds should be learning to play with friends, hearing stories in a circle at the library, collecting leaves and rocks on walks around the block that take hours. . . .

But this little three-year-old lay in a hospital bed.

As the days progressed and Michelle told me more of

Megan's diagnosis, I continued to hide my tears from her. I reasoned that my tears would not help my friend stay strong. But after a phone call, I would run for my basement where I would sit in a chair and cry and pray.

What would have happened if I had let those tears out during my conversation with Michelle? Would she have felt responsible for making me sad? Would she have felt she needed to comfort me? Would she have felt she should keep details from me?

Maybe. Or maybe not. Maybe as I cried with her on the phone we would have both found relief and release.

In the book of Lamentations, Jeremiah talks openly about his tears. In fact, before he gets to the verse that Michelle and I love so much, "Because of the LORD's great love, we are not consumed. . . ." (3:22), he spends two chapters telling God about his sorrow: "This is why I weep and my eyes overflow with tears" (1:16).

Clearly Jeremiah didn't stay stuck in his tears, but he also did not try to pretend them away.

Learning to Embrace Tears

Many months after my tear-inducing conversations with Michelle, I continued to struggle with what to do with tears as I faced my mom's illness.

Late in December 2005 I flew home to hug my kids and husband and to sleep. My brothers joined forces with Mom's friends to try caring for her in her own home. But soon we all began to realize that Mom needed more help than we could give. Once again, her friends listened to our concerns, shared their concerns, and offered their physical and emotional support.

> *How very painful this is. We all know that your mom takes great strength from being in her home, but this might not be possible. I will help you in reinforcing for your mom any decision that you feel is necessary.*
> *—Judy L*

Shortly after Christmas, Joe found a room for Mom at a care facility and with lots of help moved her in. How he negotiated all of this with Mom and her doctors and other caregivers I will never fully know.

When I saw Mom next, she sat in her favorite chair next to a large window that looked out at the Colorado foothills. She was sobbing. A woman I had never met sat holding Mom in a gentle hug. Clearly, she had spent time crying too. *How should I respond? Oh, what an awkward moment!*

My mom's friend said, "We were just having a good cry together."

I had done most of my crying, especially lately, alone at night, buried under a pile of blankets. I smiled weakly and sat down. *Crying together? A good thing?* I thought to myself. *Isn't the chin-up, look-at-the-bright-side approach more uplifting? Or did I miss something by keeping my tears to myself?*

Many years earlier I had memorized a Bible verse in the King James Version that now floated back into my head: "Rejoice with them that do rejoice, and weep with them that weep" (Romans 12:15, KJV). *The Message* says it this way: "Laugh with your happy friends when they're happy; share tears when they're down."

What did my mom need? What did I need? Tears?

Several days later, the friend who had wept with Mom came back for a visit.

"We lost our daughter, Abby, a few years ago," Christy

said. "Your mom was always so kind to us and to Abby."

I remembered Mom mentioning Abby, a delightful little girl she had come to know through her job as a children's librarian. Abby had been born with severe disabilities and could not walk or talk. She defied doctors' odds by living ten years.

How do you respond when a friend weeps in your presence?

Had Mom wept with Christy years earlier? Whether or not tears fell from her eyes, I know she wept internally as her heart filled with sorrow. She felt this family's pain. I know she expressed it with her eyes, her mouth, and her hands.

I would guess that Mom delivered homemade chocolate chip cookies and flowers from her garden to Christy's family. I would guess that she held Abby's hand and smiled at her. I know she prayed.

And now Christy came. She filled Mom's room with the music that had so touched her daughter's soul. And she wept. Her music, her presence, and her tears—all gifts. All ways to say, "I care. I see your pain. I see you."

Perhaps the true gift of tears lies in the washing away of the veneer on our eyes that keeps us from seeing deep pain.

Weeping Turned to Joy

After Christy left the nursing home that first day, I sat with Mom and listened to her halting speech interspersed with her tears.

"This is hard. My brain! Oh . . . doing its own thing!"

"Oh, Mom. It is hard. It is. Your brain is wacky."

Then Mom stared at me and asked me a question I did not expect: "Am I dying?"

I hesitated, unsure how I should respond. No one had ever asked me this question before. I had just gotten off an airplane and truthfully I really longed for a nap. "No," I responded slowly. "Not that I know of. I just came to say hello and see your new room."

How do you respond to sorrow? Do you stuff your tears? Do you let others see them? Do you take them to God?

I knew that Mom knew her prognosis. Or did she? Her brain had become so unreliable. I rationalized my avoidance to myself. *How would talking of death make her feel better? Will she even understand what I say?* Her sorrow seemed to shake her whole being. I so did not want to add to that sorrow.

"Yes, you are dying," sounded so final. So factual. So cold. So not-encouraging. I forced a smile and said what I thought Mom would like to hear.

I often replay that scene in my head and wonder what would have happened if I had said instead, "Yes, Mom. You are dying." Would she have let out a piercing scream? Would she have refused to let me visit again? Would I have lost my composure and cried in loud sobs that upset Mom even more? Truth and tears have an intricate connection.

Wise King Solomon had such a clear sense of the rhythms of life: "There is a time for everything, and a season for every activity under the heavens . . . a time to be born and a time to die . . . a time to weep and a time to laugh. . . ." (Ecclesiastes 3:1,4, NIV).

So when is the time to talk of death?

After Mom had wept awhile that day, I asked her a question. "Mom, do you think about heaven? What do you think it will be like?"

"Music," she said. "Beautiful music."

I nodded. "Just imagine all the voices singing."

"And pink. Do you think heaven will be pink?"

I couldn't help but laugh. Pink? In heaven? I knew that Mom had read the same verses in the Bible that I had—all of which described heaven in shades of gold. I also knew that pink had never been on Mom's list of favorite colors. But now, thinking of heaven as pink brought a smile to both of our faces.

As we continued to talk of possible colors in heaven and a place brimming with music, Mom's sobbing gradually stopped and her face and body began to relax. We sat quietly and looked out her window at the bright blue sky and majestic Colorado foothills, and let our minds and hearts turn to thinking about the joy on the other side of this world, the joy of heaven.

Had I cut short Mom's time of grieving? Perhaps. Had I pushed aside her tears in my need to feel some sense of hope? Perhaps. Had I kept too tight a reign on my own tears? Perhaps.

I could not imagine walking away from Mom that day and leaving her to shake in sorrow. I longed to give her hope, to dry her tears. I could not offer her the hope of medication that would cure her wacky brain. And I could not promise her sorrow-free days ahead. I could, however, remind her of the hope of heaven.

Weeping and joy seem so interconnected, almost two sides of a coin. David said it so well in Psalm 30:5:

"weeping may endure for a night, but joy cometh in the morning" (KJV).

What If?

Dying and living, weeping and laughing—all parts of our existence here on earth. What would happen in your friendships if together you embraced the hard parts of life and did not fear weeping together?

Chapter 6

Helping in
Tangible Ways

Toilet paper, toothpaste, frozen pizza, frozen dinners, snacks for school lunches. . . . Every time I made a trip to Colorado to see Mom, I tried to leave my family stocked with the essentials. I had come to realize that I might not return when I thought I would, and I wanted to save my husband constant runs to the grocery store in between his full-time day job and his full-time evening Dad-job.

Michelle emailed frequently. One day she said, "I am taking your family dinner tonight. It makes me feel better. . . ."

I smiled when I read that email and knew that it would also make my family feel better. Sure, they could feed themselves. If necessary, they could live on frozen pizzas. But just having Michelle show up with a dinner would remind them that we were not isolated in our storm. Other people knew and cared.

I also smiled at Michelle's insight that she would feel better by helping. I knew that her heart ached for my family who had given me up for so many weeks. I knew that as she cooked, she prayed. She needed, and wanted, to DO something.

Michelle could just as easily have delivered a dinner she purchased at the grocery store, local deli, or fast food restaurant. She could have ordered pizza for delivery. She chose to cook a dinner and deliver it because she liked doing that.

Giving a tangible gift of love and support, something that smells good, tastes incredible, looks beautiful, or feels soft and comforting, can fill any storm with a bit of unexpected joy. And who of us does not need that glimpse of joy on a dark, dark day?

Honestly, cooking for someone else just isn't at the top of my bringing-comfort-to-others list. I can find my way around my kitchen, but I have also made some memorable kitchen mistakes, such as forgetting to add cooking oil to a boxed brownie mix! I can laugh now about serving brick-hard brownies to a group of students.

So, when Michelle hit her storm with Megan, long before I hit my storm with my mom, my first response to help her in a tangible way did not include a home-cooked meal. As we talked on the phone one day, I realized that Michelle had given up going to her weekly Bible study because it happened the day after Megan had her chemotherapy. Michelle could not take Megan and risk exposing her to infection. I knew that my friend, an extrovert, would gain strength and joy from spending a few hours with other women studying the Bible.

"How about if I come over on Wednesday mornings and hang out with Megan? That way you can go to Bible study."

"Really?"

"Yes, really. Please go. It would make me happy."

And so for a series of Wednesday mornings, I spent a few hours sitting close to a very tired three-year-old. We covered ourselves with blankets and sank into Michelle's living room sofa to read books and play with stuffed animals. Between stories we sometimes talked a bit about what had happened the day before.

When I returned home after my Megan-mornings, I noticed that I felt unusually at peace. What a surprise! I expected to feel stressed about the laundry I hadn't done that morning or the emails and phone calls I hadn't answered. Instead, I smiled. After all, I had just spent a few hours doing something I truly enjoy—sitting and listening and reading.

"Ready!"

As I watched my mother's friends surround her in Colorado, I marveled at the things they thought to do.

Mom had "700 friends" long before the days of Facebook. It happened as she lived and worked as a children's librarian in the same town for almost fifty years. I remember walking through the grocery store with her when I came home from college and seeing an excited child point at Mom and shout, "Look! It's the library!"

Overwhelmed at the thought of trying to connect with so many people when her brain would not do what she wanted it to do, Mom asked that we limit the number of people who came to see her. And so Team Nancy developed.

These friends knew Mom, and they knew what would bring her joy. They had gone to operas together, shared lunches, cups of tea, honest discussions, and family stories and photos. Over the years they had listened and watched. They would not, could not, stop now. Team Nancy suited up.

One friend suggested keeping a journal for visitors to record their observations. Another suggested hanging a white board and writing down the visiting schedule so that everyone, including staff, could see it. Another friend retrieved some of Mom's favorite clothes from her house.

Like a choreographed dance, each person took a role and performed it with grace and strength, creating something of breathtaking beauty.

"I feel so fortunate to be witness to so many good, caring people working through difficult issues. . . . it certainly makes one lose his/her cynicism," wrote one member of Team Nancy in an email.

Team Nancy also thought of ways to help that I had never imagined.

Jim and I offered to get Nancy's house prepared to be unoccupied. We planned to clean out the refrigerator, turn off water, etc. We were also going to find homes for the plants, but if someone else wants them or wants to do that or anything else, just let me know. . . . We do have keys, and I would be happy to take things to Nancy or to loan my key should someone else want to get items for her.

By doing these practical tasks, Mom's friends gave our brains and hearts some relief from the daily flood of details, They gave us time to focus on how best to care for Mom, and they gave us some time to do something for ourselves, such as sleep.

Doing and caring—so intertwined.

Helping a Storm Sister through a stormy period might mean walking her dog, folding her laundry, making a grocery run, taking her turn in the neighborhood carpool, mopping her kitchen floor, mowing her yard, scrubbing the mold out of her shower, developing a filing system for important papers, answering emails for her. . . .

Each task speaks just as loudly as a thoughtful sympathy card. Maybe louder.

The Bible continually challenges us to put feet and

Many women struggle with connecting to others, especially in times of struggle. Spend some time now thinking and praying about how you run to or run away from others during storms.

arms to our faith by helping others: "Suppose a brother or a sister is without clothes and daily food. If one of you says to them, 'Go in peace; keep warm and well fed,' but does nothing about their physical needs, what good is it?" (James 2:15-16, NIV).

Just Doing What Needs Doing

It was only about six weeks ago your mother and I were having lunch and talking about the future. And it was only several months ago you and I were hatching plans for a 70th birthday celebration. . . .

Judy had a gift for hatching events involving my mom— a retirement party, holiday gatherings, birthday events. . . . And now one of those hoped-for celebrations had turned with lightning speed into a farewell event, fraught with sorrow.

I knew that Judy had two adult daughters, a husband, and a full-time job full of responsibility. And yet, she continued to do all that she could for Mom.

In an email to my brothers and me she wrote simply, "My last two visits with your mother had to be in the early evening. . . . Both times I have been able to feed her and help her get ready for bed."

Her words painted with broad strokes a situation that actually played out as anything but straightforward and easy. I knew that Judy usually arrived after sunset, which meant that she saw Mom at her most confused and agitated. When sunset came, Mom also seemed to set somehow. I also knew that when dinner arrived, Mom would make her most gallant efforts to feed herself in front of her friend.

How easy it would have been for Judy to smile politely, offer a quick hug, and say that she needed to get home to see her husband. She didn't do that. And she didn't demand that a nurse step in and help. She also didn't ignore Mom's dinner getting cold in front of her. She reached down and picked up some food on a fork and extended it to Mom's mouth. Just as if they sat chatting at one of their frequent lunches over the years. What a clear illustration to me of Matthew 25:40: "Whatever you did for one of the least of these brothers and sisters of mine, you did for me" (NIV).

What If?

"How can I help?" How many times do we ask that question? What if instead of asking that question, you said to a hurting friend, "I would like to drive your kids to school this week," or "I'm coming over to do your cleaning and laundry on Tuesday."

Chapter 7

Respecting Limits

At the onset of Michelle's daughter's disease and before Mom's illness, I willingly stepped into Michelle's world and tried to keep it running for a few days while Michelle and her husband sorted out medical issues.

After dinner at our house on day two, I headed out the door with Michelle's young son, Calvin, so he could sleep at his house. My wise husband pulled me aside and said quietly, "You can't do it all. Don't try." I simply smiled and nodded my head. *I can. I can do it all. I know I can.*

That night after I tucked Calvin in bed, Michelle's phone started ringing. "Hi. This is Ryan's mom. We can't reach Ryan. Do you know what is going on?" I explained all I knew and tried to sound reassuring.

Michelle's mom called next: "I can't reach Michelle.

Do you know anything?" Again, I tried to offer words of comfort. Minutes after I said good-bye to Michelle's mom, Michelle's brother called.

When the phone rang for the fourth time, I surprisingly heard the voice of my friend, Karyn, on the other end. "You sound exhausted. How about if I come over for the night?"

Before I could answer her, my cell phone rang. Michelle began to cry on the other end, "I'm so tired. I can hardly breathe."

I tried to say something comforting before I hung up the phone. *Why did I feel so sad and tired? Certainly I could will myself to do what needed doing for a few days.*

Maybe. Or maybe I needed to acknowledge my fatigue and longing to sleep in my own bed. By trying to do more than I could, did I think I could fill in for God? When Job struggled to find God in his suffering and struggled to believe that God was truly in control, God reminded him: "Is it your wisdom that makes the hawk soar and spread its wings toward the south?" (Job 39:26, NLT).

Gradually, I realized my husband had spoken truth to me. I couldn't do it all.

Military leaders know that one person cannot accomplish nearly what a group of organized people can.

The dramatic Old Testament story of Elisha speaks so clearly to the power of marshaling the troops:

> *When the servant of the man of God got up and went out early the next morning, an army with horses and chariots had surrounded the city. "Oh no, my lord! What shall we do?" the servant asked.*
>
> *"Don't be afraid," the prophet answered. "Those who are with us are more than those who are with them."*
>
> *And Elisha prayed, "Open his eyes, Lord, so that he may see." Then the Lord opened the servant's eyes, and he looked and saw the hills full of horses and chariots of fire all around Elisha* (2 Kings 6:15-17, NIV).

When I finished talking to Michelle on the phone that night, I knew I had to "marshal the troops."

I called a pastor at our church, also Michelle's church. "Hi, Marc. I just got off the phone with my good friend, Michelle." Marc listened carefully as I poured out my story to him. "Could you call Michelle?"

"Sure. I will call her right now. But, Afton, we also need

How easily do you recognize your limits? What pushes you to marshal the troops on earth and in heaven?

to figure out a way to get you some help. Write down a list of Michelle's friends. I know Pam is one of them. You are going to have to make phone calls. You can't carry this yourself, Afton."

Marc's direct words challenged me, something I did not expect. I had called him to get help for my friend, not for myself. Marc gave me permission to admit that I did not have to be a super friend who could do everything for my suffering friend.

So I marshaled my second troop: "Karyn, would you still be up for coming over to stay with Calvin tonight? You're right. I do feel exhausted."

Owning Personal Limits

When I offered to help Michelle, I jumped in with both feet, attempting to mount a single-handed rescue operation. Now, months later, I watched as my mother's friends assembled and did just the opposite.

Each day will be new, I am sure. We will have to see how Nancy adjusts, and what her needs are. That means we will communicate a lot, I am sure. Just know that I am delighted to be working with such a wonderful team of folks who love Nancy.

—Judy L

These women seemed to instinctively know that this needed to be a shared task—for their own sake as well as for Mom's best interests. No solo acts of rescuing here.

They did what they could, when they could, and then they let someone else step in and do the same.

Earlier this evening I talked to Judy M about getting some people organized to be with Nancy. She is already lining this up! I told her I would help with the list for January, and I could easily check with Nancy on Mondays, Wednesdays, and Fridays if she could find folks to come in on Tuesdays and Thursdays, which are not as good for me. . . . I must admit that this weekend is really frantic for me, with all family home, and party, etc. However, on Monday my schedule is much more flexible.

—Judy L

These women knew their limits. And felt okay about admitting them to me and to each other. By doing so they did not pretend to be something they were not—superwomen, and they made room for a cohesive, strong, interdependent team to develop.

Voicing Limits

I wanted everyone to feel happy. I wanted everyone to see Mom and say good-bye in person. I wanted Mom to sense how many people deeply cared about her. But Mom had asked us to limit her visitors to only a small circle.

One night as I tossed and turned, I wrestled with different ideas for helping Mom's friends grieve her inevitable death. Cards. Flowers. . . . Nothing seemed grand enough or permanent enough.

Then I remembered Peggy and her beautiful quilts. I smiled to myself at the idea of people signing a square and then having Peggy sew them into a quilt for Mom. I drifted off to sleep. The next morning, I sent an email to Peggy outlining my clever idea. She responded graciously.

I hope that you will come over to my house at some point, and we can discuss getting something together for Nancy's friends to sign. A signature quilt, while a wonderful idea, is a huge undertaking of time, and I don't think it is a do-able project under the circumstances. But we could talk about a small throw or large pillow to accommodate a number of the signatures of her friends.

We all wanted to do something grand and beautiful to help Mom. But none of us could do the most grand and beautiful thing of all—keep her from death.

I imagine that Peggy struggled to write that email, but I will forever be glad that she did.

Her response reminded me that I had limits too. I needed to say to myself and to others, "I can't do that." I could not single-handedly keep everyone happy and grieving well.

Jesus said it so well in His Sermon on the Mount, where He spoke of heart-attitudes and tips

When have you said, "Yes" when you really should have said, "No"? What might have happened if you had simply said, "No. I'm sorry, but I can't"?

for daily living: "All you need to say is simply 'Yes' or 'No'" (Matthew 5:37, NIV).

Recognizing Physical Limits

Mom developed a theory.

She believed that if she did not sleep for more than two hours at a time her brain would not go into its uncooperative funk as often. So she directed the night nursing staff at the care facility to wake her up every two hours.

I decided to spend a night with Mom early in her experiment so that I could see firsthand how her theory played out. After we tucked her in and turned out the lights, I lay quietly and listened for that settled breathing that indicated Mom had drifted into sleep. Almost forty-five minutes elapsed. Then in just over an hour, the staff came to wake Mom up. After several cycles of this, I realized that Mom had hardly slept. At some point in the night, I quietly said to the staff, "Let's let her sleep for at least four hours."

When the next evening arrived, I thought of spending another night with Mom. And yet, I so longed for a night of uninterrupted sleep. Selfish? Should I just ignore the ache behind my eyes, drink another cup of coffee, and carry on? I wanted to be kind. I wanted to help. I wanted to do what a daughter should do for her dying mother.

As I contemplated what to do, the hospice team and care facility staff appeared, as if from thin air. They circled around me and spoke truth to me: "You look so tired. You need to get some rest. We are here."

I listened to them and to my aching head telling me to slow down. The next morning, someone on staff said, "You must have gotten some sleep. You look so much better."

What If?

We women tend to think that we have to do it all for everyone. What would happen if we gave each other permission to say, "I recognize my limits in this situation. I can't . . . "?

Chapter 8

Offering and Accepting
Wise Counsel

Move over, Dear Abby.

For an assignment in a high school journalism class, I wrote an advice column. I don't remember the problem, and I don't remember my solution, but I do remember the exhilaration I felt as I poured out my sixteen years of wisdom. Maybe someday I could have my own advice column. . . .

And then I grew older and discovered some of the rough patches in life and realized that, in truth, I was the one who needed advice. So as I walked through my mother's illness, I sought out women I knew could give me wise counsel. These women had navigated tough times in their own lives with faith and grace. Not with perfection. And not without pain.

One of the women I sought out taught me piano during my high school years. Although I had not taken lessons from her for years, we stayed in touch by sending Christmas cards, and I popped in to see her when I came home. She had been such a down-to-earth voice of kindness, faith, and wisdom during my challenging teenage years. (And she thought she was just teaching me to play the piano!)

How do you pick wise friends? How do you respond to the advice you receive from these women? And how do you know when to offer wisdom gracefully?

This woman willingly stepped back into my life again when I arrived in Colorado to help my mom. She kidnapped me for lunch one day, helped me put together the music for Mom's memorial service, and sent me notes, one of which contained these wise words:

Praise God for a beautiful life lived to the fullest. Praise God for His eternal home where there is no pain or suffering. Praise God for family and friends. Praise God from whom all blessings flow.

When we walk the narrow path, we stumble and fall and meet challenges that overwhelm us and

feel painful, but there is always a gentle hand to help
us along the way.

The Power of Wise Counsel

I always wanted a sister. Someone to share clothes with, braid each other's hair, fight over the same boy. . . .

When I married my husband twenty-seven years ago, my wish came partially true when I got to know his two sisters. We didn't fight over the same boy (!), but we did, and still do, explore thrift stores, celebrate birthdays, get the giggles over a crazy shopping story, and wipe the tears from our eyes as we talk about life's struggles.

As I flew back and forth to Colorado, I knew that their hearts ached with me and that they prayed for me daily.

During one of my stints in Colorado, one of my sisters-in-law sent me a letter full of kindness and concern (and a tea bag!), but also full of wise counsel.

> *. . . I was thinking about the fact that you have a*
> *lot of eyes on you these days Afton—your kids, your*
> *siblings, all watching how you are responding to this.*

Then the verses from Hebrews 12:1-3 came to mind of the other great crowd of witnesses you have watching you: "Therefore, since we are surrounded by such a great cloud of witnesses, let us throw off everything that hinders and the sin that so easily entangles. And let us run with perseverance the race marked out for us, fixing our eyes on Jesus, the pioneer and perfecter of faith. For the joy set before him he endured the cross, scorning its shame, and sat down at the right hand of the throne of God. Consider him who endured such opposition from sinners, so that you will not grow weary and lose heart."

Take one day at a time, take time for yourself, and know we are praying for you!

Love you! Ellen

Wise counsel. Such perspective-giving, courage-building wise counsel. What a gift.

The Wisdom of "Been There"

Way back in high school, a friend of mine lost her father suddenly, I think to a heart attack. I remember feeling sad. I remember going to the funeral. I probably sent a card. But once my friend returned to school, I remember being afraid to say anything to her. Would I make her more sad? Death had not become part of my vocabulary at that point.

Now, decades later, I found myself immersed in death. Mom's fatal disease took me by complete surprise. I felt as if I were on a playground merry-go-round and just trying to hang on for the ride.

I had admired from a distance how my childhood friend Roberta left her young family to go and sit with her father in his last days. Now, in my dizziness, she, too, spoke words of wise counsel.

Dear Afton, I pray that you and your mom have some quality time together during your visit. Spend some time doing something that you know will bring comfort to both of you—praying, reading from one of C.S. Lewis' books, sharing some artwork that your kids have done, eating a hot fudge sundae, looking at photos or a video of your family activities. I know that there are lots of loose ends that you need to deal with, too, but put the focus on the relationship if you can.

—Prayers, Roberta

Roberta's advice helped me stop spinning. Frankly, my instinct pushed me to stay busy with details. I now forced myself to sit. Sometimes Mom and I could share a story or conversation, but often her brain just couldn't function well enough to focus on anything. So I sat. And I prayed.

What causes you to hesitate offering wise counsel, bathed in prayer, to a struggling friend? What causes you to hesitate accepting wise counsel from a Storm Sister?

We can learn so much from a friend who has been there. King Solomon said it well: "Get all the advice and instruction you can, so you will be wise the rest of your life" (Proverbs 19:20, NLT).

The Right Words at the Right Time

My mother loved to travel and read. Those two passions meshed perfectly when she traveled twice to England with a group sponsored by the Marion E. Wade Center, a research collection of works by and about seven well-known British authors, including C.S. Lewis and J.R.R. Tolkien.

True to form, Mom made friends on the trips, including Marj, the associate director. So when Mom came to visit me, she always set up a time to have a cup of tea with Marj at her office a few blocks away. When Mom became ill, I knew that I had to contact Marj.

Marj's reply to my email, full of her gentle wisdom and kindness, reminded me that Mom loved English choral music—something I had forgotten. But she said far more than that.

I'll look forward to hearing from you as to where and when your mother would feel up to a phone call. But please don't feel any pressure on that account. I understand the realities you are wrestling with at the moment. Don't neglect taking care of yourself as you

struggle through these difficult days. Your mother would want you to do so. She loves you very much.
—With my ongoing prayers, Marj

By the time Marj wrote this note, Mom had lost much of her immense vocabulary. She had also lost the voice of her heart. She couldn't describe her emotions, and she couldn't tell me that she loved me. Something I so needed to hear.

How and when do you speak words of wise counsel to a friend? How do you muster the courage?

Not knowing any of this, Mom's friend stepped in and became my mother's voice for a brief moment, a moment I needed desperately.

"She loves you very much."

I still marvel that Marj had the courage and wisdom to write these heart-healing words to me at just the right time, living out the truth of Proverbs 25:11: "A word fitly spoken is like apples of gold in pictures of silver" (KJV).

The Goodness of God's Wise Counsel

As I continued to pass the days by my mom's side, I sent the following email update to family and Storm Sisters:

Just a quick update. I am still in Colorado. As of today Mom is on both an anti-anxiety drug and regular doses of morphine. She is now in pain. She says her whole body hurts.

As I sit with her and listen to music or just sit in silence, I pray that soon God's angels will escort her to heaven where she will be able to sing again.

That, in turn, prompted a short email from Michelle:

Dearest Afton,
My prayers and thoughts are with you. Hang on to God's goodness. . . .
Love you! Michelle

I knew exactly what Michelle meant. Months earlier we had talked about her daughter's illness and the many unknowns. Would the chemotherapy work? Would sweet little

Megan lose her hair? What happened if Megan got a cold and couldn't have chemo?

That morning, over coffee, I gently reminded Michelle of a truth I had been savoring: "I remain confident of this: I will see the goodness of the Lord in the land of the living. Wait for the Lord; be strong and take heart and wait for the Lord" (Psalm 27:13-14, NIV).

"Michelle," I said. "You will see the goodness of God in all of this. I know you will. Take heart."

And now, my friend, in her shorthand, reminded me of this truth, one she knew that I knew and believed: God is good. Always. Even in the darkest, most uncertain days. So why did she remind me? Because she also understood that memory and belief can so easily fade in times of stress.

Michelle knew me well enough to know how much I love the Psalms, and she, no doubt, sensed from the tone of this email and others that I struggled to hang on to God.

Take heart. Wait for the Lord. God is good.

What If?

We gather advice from so many venues—the internet, family traditions, friends, books. . . . Do you know a woman who seems truly wise? What if you approached her and asked if you could meet monthly?

Chapter 9

Sharing Important Events

Elizabeth, like Roberta, knew me in the days of acne and braces. At our weekly high school girls' Bible studies, she asked probing questions and listened to my many questions. Later in life, I talked to her about finding the right husband, coping with my parents' divorce, my love of British literature. . . .

Elizabeth, now an empty-nester, offered me a bed at any time during my mom's illness. I explained to her in an email, "At the moment I'm okay by myself at Mom's house. It seems nice to be here. I think, though, that once she leaves this world for the next one, I would love to come spend a night or two at your house."

The day after I wrote that email to Elizabeth, my mom slipped gently from this world and entered a world where her brain could no longer derail her. A world so beautiful I cannot even hope to imagine it. God's world. Heaven.

I called Elizabeth. "My mom slipped away to heaven tonight," I explained as my voice gave out. "My oldest brother is here with me, but could I come spend the night in your Pink Rose Room? I'm so tired."

How would you respond to a last-minute request of help?

And so that night I fell into a bed with soft pillows and comforters in a room beautifully decorated with antiques and roses. I cried and prayed and let go.

When Elizabeth invested herself in my high-school self, she could not have had any inkling that I would call her decades later on a cold January night asking for a bed and a place to cry. But when I asked, she did not shirk from walking through this key moment in my life with me. It seems that somewhere, during high school and beyond, we had become Storm Sisters.

Showing Up

Planning a Thanksgiving menu, buying and wrapping Christmas gifts, and now planning a memorial service—all in the space of three months. No wonder I felt as if I walked in a constant fog.

As my husband made plans to fly out to Colorado with our kids for Mom's memorial service, he got a phone call from his sister Ellen: "I'm looking into flights for the memorial service. Do you know yet when it is?"

My mother had often participated in celebrations that also involved my husband's family. She loved the Norwegian Christmas traditions we celebrated together, and she told me more than once how glad she felt that I married into such a kind family. And now Ellen wanted once again to weave our families together.

Mom would have been so delighted. In a beautifully written obituary, my brother Joe explained it all so well:

> . . . *In the three months of her illness, Nancy was constantly surrounded by her family and her extensive community of friends. As we all understand the depth of her love and involvement with so many*

people, it's clear that her largest knitting project is now complete—a beautiful tapestry of people connected with one another. She must be very pleased.

I know it wasn't easy for Ellen to make that trip. It took planning, effort, time, and money. I had no idea then how much it would mean to me years later when I could make reference to that immense day and see Ellen nod her head. She understood. She was present.

Ellen lived out for me these words of Paul: "So let's not allow ourselves to get fatigued doing good. At the right time we will harvest a good crop if we don't give up, or quit. Right now, therefore, every time we get the chance, let us work for the benefit of all, starting with the people closest to us in the community of faith" (Galatians 6:9–10, *The Message*).

Why not send a note (or a batch of cookies) today to a woman in your life who has invested time in you? If this woman has left this world, send a note to her family.

Another woman, the mother of my longtime friend Roberta also showed up at my mom's memorial service.

Roberta and I, in our days of learning to cook and messing around (or messing up) a kitchen, made many a batch of "Dirty

Cookies"—a family recipe handed down from my great-grandmother. Family legend states that Gam liked to make these cookies with her granddaughter, Nancy, my mom. My mom dubbed them "Dirty Cookies" because of the chocolate chunks in them.

So . . . it should not have surprised me when Roberta's mom showed up at Mom's memorial service, with a batch of "Dirty Cookies" for the reception. Of course!

In a card a few days later, Roberta sent her own memorial of my mom.

Your mom had a wonderful group of friends and family, and we are blessed to be among them. My kids remember her as the "story lady," and each of them has a pair of knitted booties courtesy of Mrs. Banks. I appreciated her sharing her list of favorite children's books over the years. . . .

Although we were not physically there, we were lifting your family up in prayer each day. Being with someone at the end of their days on earth is such a gift, and Afton, I know how courageous you were to be able to be with your mom these past couple of weeks as her health declined. . . .

I have so many memories of your family during the years we were in junior high and high school, and I'm so glad that we have remained friends over the years.

—*Love and blessings, Berta*

Roberta's words, thankful words for the time my mom had invested in her, remind me of these words from 1 Thessalonians 1:2–3: "We always thank God for all of you and continually mention you in our prayers. We remember before our God and Father your work produced by faith, your labor prompted by love, and your endurance inspired by hope in our Lord Jesus Christ" (NIV).

Remembering Birthdays

I don't think I have ever laughed as hard with a friend as I did with Kim. It seemed anything could set us off. Baking cookies (yes, "Dirty Cookies") from dough that we had dropped on the floor and then serving them to our older brothers. . . . Trying to ride our bikes while wearing those pants with beyond-enormous bell-bottoms. . . .

But Kim also knew the parts of my life that did not make me laugh. She shared her room with me one night when my father's violent tantrum forced us to flee our home. She attended my father's funeral and cried with me as I spoke about this man I had worked hard to forgive.

Every year for as long as I can remember Kim and her mom baked my mom a lemon-meringue pie and delivered it to her on her birthday.

The year that mom died would have been her 70th birthday. As the day approached I couldn't help but feel sad. Although she didn't make a pie, my friend Kim sent me a card that year that tasted almost as good:

> *Dear Afton, celebrating with you your precious mom and her 70th birthday in heaven. What a glorious celebration! I'm sure your mom has every angel and every saint proficient in knitting by now. I know you miss her. I find myself missing your mom each time I pass by her neighborhood. . . . I can always hear her laughing.*

I began to laugh. Once again, my friend had helped me find my way to joy.

Saying Goodbye

By the time I returned home from Mom's memorial service, Michelle had started trying to get her parents into a care facility. Her dad had become increasingly ill even as Megan traveled to and from the hospital. He needed care and not to have to worry about maintaining a house and a yard.

Then, just months later, Michelle began to clean out her parents' house in preparation to sell it—just as my brothers and I had done a few months earlier. We talked about boxes, storage, realtors. . . .

And then, she too faced planning a memorial service for her dad. How do you capture in a five-minute, or even a ten-minute speech, the life of a parent and the relationship you shared? How do you communicate all of the memories you have to people who did not grow up with your parent? How do you honor someone with mere words?

"I promised to speak at my Dad's memorial service. Could I read you what I wrote?"

So I listened as Michelle read me her words about her father, which included a story about a little purse she cherished and how her dad took the time to say to her, "Tell me about your purse." He cared about what she cared about.

"Michelle, that story tells it all. What a beautiful picture. Focus on that."

Days later, I drove a couple of hours with other friends and listened to Michelle, in a strong voice, talk about her purse and all that it represented. Being present that day, just as so many had been present with me months earlier, opened my eyes to tears again, but it also brought me face-to-face with heaven again. I worshipped—a gift I did not expect from simply being present.

What If?

Think about the hard and wonderful events you have experienced this past year. Did you have a friend present with you at these events? What would it have meant to you to have a friend by your side?

Chapter 10

Making Time to Listen

"How are you?"

Hearing that question after my mother's death thrust me into a world of internal questions.

- *Do you really want to hear about my current fog-like state of grief?*
- *And what about the tears that erupt out of nowhere and at awkward times?*
- *How much detail should I offer?*
- *When should I turn the conversation to your life?*
- *Do I really have words for what I have just lived through?*
- *What should I tell you and what should I tell a counselor?*

- *I pour out my heart to God, but what difference will it make to do that with you?*

Sometimes I simply couldn't help myself, and words poured out of my heart before I had time to question them or rein them in. Sometimes I could see a look of shock or pain on a friend's face so I stopped the flow. Sometimes a friend quickly changed the subject so I let it rest. Sometimes I simply sat in silence and waited for a visual or verbal cue.

Several weeks after I returned from Mom's memorial service, a friend who had followed my emails and responded to them with encouraging words invited me to lunch. I agreed although I did have to drag myself there with legs that felt so heavy.

I don't remember what I ate that day, and I don't remember much of what I said or what Mary said. I do remember Mary's eyes. She looked at me as if to say, "Keep talking. I truly want to hear." And listen she did—for two hours!

I knew that Mary had days packed with work and ministry, and yet she gave me her ears and eyes for such a big chunk of her day. She lived out for me the wise words of James 1:19:

"My dear brothers and sisters, take note of this: Everyone should be quick to listen, slow to speak and slow to become angry" (NIV).

Just over a week after we celebrated Mom's life in a memorial service, her friend Marj at the Wade Center just blocks from my house sent me a kind email.

I would love to see you whenever you feel up to it. I am in the office tomorrow (Tuesday) and also Thursday and Friday. . . . In the meantime, I continue to pray for you and your family.
—Blessings, Marj

When I eventually stepped into Marj's office, I brought with me a few of Mom's CDs and books—ones I thought she might enjoy having—and a copy of the memorial service. I expected to have a short conversation, maybe a polite cup of tea, and a hug goodbye. Instead, Marj invited me to settle into her comfortable chair and tell her about my last days with her friend, my mother.

Once again, a friend listened. . . . To a story fraught with sadness.

Before long, tears began to fall from my eyes and into my mug of tea. Marj asked a few questions, nodded her head often, offered me a box of tissues, and used one herself. Like Mary, Marj had a full life of responsibilities, including a book deadline. But that afternoon, she simply sat and looked and listened.

"Can I pray for you?" she asked as my tears began to dry.

In her sun-filled office full of books by authors my mother and I both loved, Marj blessed me with tender words of prayer. Her compassionate words fell over me like a blanket of comfort as she spoke to her intimate Friend, God, about me and my family and the life and death of my mom.

Listening that turned to prayer. As naturally as reaching for a tissue to dry a tear.

When to Seek a Professional Listener

Needy.

Did I have a sign around my neck? I felt like it. Grief had made me needy. I needed friends who listened; I needed time to sleep, free of nightmare dreams of trying to rescue my mom; I needed music that lifted my spirits; I needed to walk outside; I needed to enjoy a quiet cup of flavored decaf coffee; I needed to wake up in my own bed; I needed to talk to my husband about the little nothings of life.

Where do you fall on the spectrum of listening and talking when you get together with a friend?

It took a wise counselor to help me recognize my needs. When I went to see her, something Marj had suggested I consider, I could not even remember what I loved to do before Mom's illness. I had given so much of myself to the process of being with my mom, that I had lost rather large pieces of myself.

I actually made a list of things to do that brought me joy, and then I forced myself to do one of them each day. How silly I felt. Forcing myself to enjoy life!

The words of King Solomon rang in my head: "Hope deferred makes the heart sick, but a longing fulfilled is a tree of life" (Proverbs 13:12, NIV). I needed, more than anything, hope for the future—my future that no longer included my mom.

Could a wise friend have given me the advice the counselor gave me? Possibly. I had talked to friends, but most of them had not grieved the loss of a loved one and most of them did not have a background in psychology that gave them insights into the grieving process. I needed help to address my general confusion about how to move on with my life. My need exceeded the abilities and expertise of my friends.

Time to call a professional.

A Time to Talk . . . or Not

Months after Mom's memorial service, a friend invited me to coffee one morning. I confess that I expected to do most of the talking one morning when I pulled into my friend's driveway. She knew that I had just buried my mom, and she had responded with kindness and support throughout the process.

As we sat down to coffee, I began to talk.

But then within minutes my friend turned the subject to her own struggle. As her words began to pour out in a steady stream, I

The next time you meet with a friend, spend some moments in prayer before you get together, asking God to nudge you to recalibrate your expectations as needed during your time with your friend.

could hear her pain. I did not know how to respond. My friend had always seemed so cheerful and competent. My mind raced. *What can I say? What can I do? Oh, I wish we had talked about this years ago.*

My heart ached too. I could have used a large dose of sympathetic listening. And, after all, I had made all this effort to come to my friend's house.

My internal questioning began again. *What do I do? Should I put aside my talking points and simply listen? Should I gently interrupt and change the subject? But then, again, maybe my friend needs comfort right here right now and for her that comfort comes from being able to talk.*

I scrambled to recalibrate to listening mode, not talking mode.

When I left my friend's house several hours later, I felt dazed and drained. *What had just happened?*

I had no idea. But I do believe that God knew and that He nudged me to change my expectations: "There is a time for everything, and a season for every activity under the heavens. . . . a time to be silent and a time to speak" (Ecclesiastes 3:1,7, NIV).

Weeks later I received a note from this friend: "Thank you so much for coming to see me that day. You will never know what our time together that day did for me and for our family."

Talking on Paper

When I sat down to process all that had happened during my mom's illness and death, I instinctively turned to writing. And as I thought about doing that, I realized that both Michelle and our mutual friend Karyn had also walked through recent storms in their own lives. Perhaps we could write together.

I brought up the idea over one of our dinners out. "What would you think about working on a book with me? I would like to call it *Storm Sisters* and talk about how our friendship help fast and even grew stronger during these past months of storms."

They agreed. I suggested some guidelines and a starting place. We all wrote as we found time. We regularly sent drafts back and forth to each other and met for dinner to discuss what to do next. Those months of writing and talking and putting pieces together spoke differently to each one of us—words of challenge, comfort, and wisdom.

Soon Karyn's busy life precluded her from continuing with our project, and then Michelle also opted to step aside to focus on other parts of her life. But by the time we agreed to stop working together, we looked different. Some of our grief scars had healed over. Some of the film covering our eyes and keeping us from seeing joy had peeled away. We stood a little straighter.

My friends invested hours listening to my quiet voice on paper. They didn't tell me I had to speak aloud: "Use your words." They understood that I write better than I talk. Not exactly something to brag about but nonetheless the truth.

They joined me in the language I love most: words on paper.

What If?

Extroverts and introverts tend to make good friends—one talks and the other listens. You extroverts, what might happen in your relationships if you consciously listened more? And you introverts, what might happen in your relationships if you worked hard to talk more?

Chapter 11

⧼⧽

Reaching across
Generations

Lemonade in September? Absolutely!

Michelle's daughter finished her chemotherapy and moved on to enjoy all that life holds for young girls, including running. Five years went by quickly and the word *remission* entered Michelle's vocabulary.

During those years, Michelle's family discovered an annual 5K run created to raise money to support research for Megan's rare disease. The whole family signed up for the race, and Michelle jumped at the chance to help raise additional funds by planning a lemonade stand for several September afternoons.

"Hey, Aftonian, I'm doing this lemonade stand to raise money for Megan's disease. Do you think you could come help me pour?"

So every September for six years now, I've helped Michelle pour lemonade. Megan always helps too. Each year as we laugh together, pour lemonade, and make change for customers, I savor the moment. Watching Megan run into the house for more cups feels like a celebration—a yearly milestone. And this year Megan won First Place in the Female Survivor category. You go, girl!

When I first met Megan, just a day old and still at the hospital, I remember looking at her tiny face and wondering what lay ahead. And as I held her I prayed that she would come to know and cling to God, no matter what came.

I don't know how long the lemonade stand will continue, and I don't know what connection I will have with Megan as she grows older. I do know, however, that I will forever cheer her on and thank God for allowing me to be part of her journey, a journey that, ironically, taught me so much about myself as well as about God's ever-present strength in times of storms.

What older women and younger women cross your path frequently? How might you connect with one of them?

The words of Psalm 145:5 speak my heart for Megan: "Generation after generation stands in awe of your work; each one tells stories of your mighty acts" (*The Message*).

The Circle Grows

One of my favorite professors in college introduced me to the works of Madeline L'Engle and Katherine Patterson. This woman also had a gift for encouraging the timid—me. She offered critique but always with a large dose of praise. Just the mix that helped me own a lifelong dream I had to become a writer.

When I first met Professor deVette in 1980, I never expected to still know her thirty years later, and certainly never expected to call her "Helen" and friend. It happened year by year as we sat in her cozy living room discussing words, writers, former students, faith in God, and life.

In October of 2005, she, my mom, and I all signed up for C.S. Lewis conference, sponsored by the Marion E. Wade Center. We eagerly anticipated hearing Katherine Patterson, one of the featured speakers, as well as an evening dinner.

The night arrived for the dinner, and we found our way

to a table. My mom chose a seat next to Katherine Patterson, while Helen and I found other seats at the same table. How like God to gather these women together and give us the gift of each other and words before one of us—my mom—lost her words.

My friend Helen deVette wrote me a kind note soon after Mom's memorial service.

> *Dearest Afton,*
> *I was saddened and surprised to hear of your mother's passing. . . . I'm grateful for that happy visit with your mom at the Lewis dinner when I was privileged to meet her. . . . I pray that you and your family will know how much we and your friends love you. Heaven is real—more so, now that your mom has joined the heavenly chorus.*
> *Much love, Helen*

Another kind note came from the mother of my best friend throughout junior high, high school, and beyond. I nicknamed this woman "Mrs. Sobie" and still think of her as my "In-town mother."

Dear Afton and family—
What a lovely "send off" for your Mom—and aren't
you glad you were able to be with her during her final
journey? Have no regrets. . . . Remember, I told you
that the Hospice where you are, as well as the one
here, offer a lot of help—just reach out for it. . . . I'm
so pleased my girls have such lovely friends as you and
that you continue to be my friend too!
—Mrs. Sobie

A few months later Mrs. Sobie also gave me a framed
needlepoint saying, a copy of one that hangs in their living
room.

Our family is a circle of strength and love. With ev-
ery birth and every union, the circle grows. Every
joy shared adds more love. Every crisis faced together
makes the circle stronger.

Family. Some genetic. Some adopted. All woven together to build courage-giving, storm-worthy strength.

Months after Mom's death and after we had sold her
home, I returned to my hometown to tie up some loose ends

and also to drive around and say goodbye to the memories I had in that town. I knew it would be a rather sad, lonely journey, so I called Mrs. Sobie and asked if I could spend the night.

"Of course! And in the morning I'll take you out for breakfast at one of my favorite places."

Now a widow, she knew what it felt like to grieve and willingly shared her grief-journey with me. We also shared a few laughs as we remembered some of my teenage moments shared with her daughter.

How might you act as "family" to someone who has no family nearby?

I left town right after that breakfast with a new, unexpected memory of time and conversation with a friend and with these words of David ringing in my head, "God sets the lonely in families. . . ." (Psalm 68:6, NIV).

Staying Connected

At Mom's memorial service four young men, gathered from various parts of the country and stood to give tribute to my mom.

In elementary school she had offered them a challenge to read hard books . . . such as those by C.S. Lewis, Lloyd Alexander, and J.R.R. Tolkien . . . and they had responded with enthusiasm. She nurtured in them a lifelong love of reading and learning, forever marking their lives.

What I didn't know was that Mom kept up with these boys long after they graduated from her library. Apparently, they often got together for tea or dinner and gifted each other with talk of words and travel, both subjects dear to mom's heart.

My mom also shared her love of books—and knitting— with two particular young women: a high school friend of one of my brothers and a high school friend of mine. One of these young women helped Mom, a recent single mom, move into her new house; the other helped my brothers clean out Mom's house after her memorial service. She also took home many balls of yarn to knit something for my youngest brother's as-yet-unborn children—a promise she made to my mom.

What motivated Mom to connect with—and stay connected to—these young men and women? I don't know. I do know that these young men and women carry with them a part of my mom—a part she gave them. And they remind me again of the power of words and time and care and concern passed from one generation to the next.

Your Friends . . . My Friends

After my mom's memorial service, my life slowly began to settle back into a new normal rhythm. But something happened that I hadn't expected.

I missed my mom's friends.

So strange to go from daily visits and conversation to now living 1,000 miles away and settling back into our own lives. I wondered what would come of us.

But these women did not forget me. Peggy regularly sent me delightful e-cards that made me laugh; Judy L. sent thoughtful notes by snail mail; Judy M. stayed in touch via e-mail. When I published a children's book, they rejoiced with me as my mother would have. And we stay in touch still—these women who showed me how to sit in the face of death.

Almost five years after Mom left this world, I sat and talked to Judy M. for a long time at the wedding of one of my nephews. We talked of her kids and grandkids, my kids, and of course Mom, her good friend. Remembering together brought both tears and joy.

After the wedding I emailed her and updated her on our family news, including our daughter fulfilling a lifelong dream to go to Europe and study. She emailed back with news of her recent travels and family and ended her message with these words:

> *It was nice to be able to see some of the family at the wedding. I don't want to ever lose touch completely because with all your mother and I shared over the years, I feel that I have a close tie to many of you.*
> *—With warmest regards, Judy*

All these generations and all these families mixed together like a thick soup. A delicious, hearty, nourishing soup.

What If?

We all interact with women of different generations—a neighbor's daughter, a niece, a grand-
mother, a mother-in-law, a college student. . . .
What might it mean to one of these women if you
intentionally spent time with her once a month?

Chapter 12

Rejoicing with Those Who Rejoice

Christmas cards.

The year my mother died they still came—full of news of growing families and happy adventures. What did I expect—that everyone I knew had shut down their lives because of my loss? Well . . . yes.

I read the first few letters that arrived in our mailbox and put a few of the included photos on the fridge. I wanted to rejoice with these friends. I did. And yet, truthfully, reading Christmas letters made me sad. Sad that I had known such sorrow while my friends had known such joy that year. My life felt dark that year. Dark and full of the details related to settling my mother's estate.

As more cards came, I let my husband open them and read them. Then I quietly stashed them without reading them. One afternoon my husband handed me a Christmas card he had just read so that I could also read it. I shook my head, headed to add it to my stashed pile, and muttered, "I can't. I just can't read this now."

I knew well the words of Romans 12:15: "Rejoice with those who rejoice; mourn with those who mourn" (NIV), but I couldn't move myself beyond the mourning part of the equation, and I felt bad. Guilty.

The word *rejoicing* sounds so cheerful when I say it. And it calls to mind so much that feels good. Who wouldn't want to rejoice, even vicariously? And yet, as I discovered, a pretty word does not necessarily represent a pretty process.

When I took down my Christmas decorations that year, I also gathered my stash of Christmas cards and put them all in the attic, telling myself that I would read the cards next year. Well . . . I never did read most of those cards that year. Or the next year when I rediscovered them mingled with Christmas decorations.

But What about My Grief?

Should I have pushed myself to read those cards and "rejoice with those who rejoice"? Had I exceeded my allotted time of grieving and feeling sad? Does grief have an expiration date? Does it go "bad" like a carton of buttermilk?

When grief took hold of me, I found that it pushed me willy-nilly in odd directions on any given day. And I often felt shrouded in fog while trying to tear a piece of it away to peek at the world going on around me. Sometimes I just let the fog settle in. Fighting it took such effort.

Meanwhile, people I knew and loved sent wedding invitations and graduation invitations. Frankly, I did not want to go to anything. Certainly people would understand.

But then my oldest brother sent his wedding invitation. A single dad for many years, he had fallen in love with a kind, thoughtful woman who had been a friend for many years. Now they wanted to begin a new life together.

Lost in my perpetual fog, I knew I should rejoice with him; I knew I should go to the ceremony; I knew I should feel glad for his happiness. My heart just couldn't, or wouldn't, respond in kind. I wanted it to. Should I give myself a pass because of grief? Didn't I still wear a grief expiration date many months, or years, away?

My head eventually talked my heart into getting on a plane.

On the day of my brother's wedding, I sat in a pew and let the music fall over me and surprisingly my mind turned to all that still remained good in this world—love, commitment, God, family . . . and at the reception, I laughed, yes, actually laughed, with family friends.

> *How have you navigated grief? How did you know when to move on?*

Grief and joy. Can they, should they, coexist? Do we have to finish our "time to weep" before we can move on to "a time to laugh" (Ecclesiastes 3:1-4, NIV)?

If only grief fit into a neat, predictable pattern. . . . If only we knew when it would end. . . .

Can We Heal by Celebrating Together?

Sorting through someone's stuff after they are gone feels, well, intrusive, wrong. And, yet, it also feels like a send-off, a wrapping-up, a way of saying, "I've got this. You go."

Every room in my mother's split-level house, including her garage, contained at least one floor-to-ceiling bookcase packed with books. And yarn and sweaters popped out of every closet. My brothers and I couldn't possibly use all of it. And, so, we did what Mom would have done—we shared.

Books, Classical CDs, Yarn, and Sweaters!
Sunday, March 12, 2006, 2-5 p.m.

As many of you know, Nancy delighted in reading, knitting, and music, but especially in sharing these things with others. In that spirit, her children invite you to come to an informal tea in her home. We'd like you to adopt the books, music, yarn, and knitted things that interest you, that most remind you of Nancy.

When the first guests arrived that Sunday afternoon, they stood uneasily in the now-empty living room. No large furniture. No crooked pictures on the wall. And no Mom sitting in her favorite rocking chair engulfed in yarn. We directed people to explore the garage, which we had turned into a library. "Grab a box or a bag and head for the garage," we urged. "Find something or several somethings you would like to adopt as a way to remember Mom."

Her church choir director gravitated to sacred music CDs. Several friends walked out wearing a sweater Mom had made. One said, "I'll finish this baby sweater for my granddaughter." Another friend called his son, currently getting his doctorate in medieval history: "I'm standing here staring at these amazing books about medieval history. And some books written in German. Would you like them?"

That Sunday afternoon we remembered Mom. Together. And we smiled. I suppose we could have kept everything ourselves in a storage locker, but Jesus' wise words urged me to do differently: "Don't store up treasures here on earth, where moths eat them and rust destroys them, and where thieves break in and steal. Store your treasures in heaven, where moths and rust cannot destroy . . ." (Matthew 6:19-20, NLT).

How might God be nudging you to use what He has given you to celebrate with a friend?

Even years after Mom's death I continued to look for ways to remember and celebrate my mother, to rejoice in the good gifts she gave me. I also looked for ways to reframe some of the challenging moments we had shared.

One fall, when Mom came for a visit, I mentioned that I had a date with John's sisters at an outlet mall for a day of bargain hunting. She grimaced. Clearly not her "thing." Hunting for a bargain at an outlet mall brings me joy. The thrill of the hunt, I guess. For my mom, hunting for a bargain at an outlet mall brought her anything but joy. And she made sure I knew that.

A few days later, however, Mom surprised me by handing me an envelope with cash peeking out of it: "Use this at the outlet mall with John's sisters. I am so glad you have them to go shopping with."

I have often thought back to that envelope (and others that followed) and my mom's generosity, her way of building a bridge between us in an area of great difference. I determined to imitate her generosity.

When the next outlet mall event with my sisters-in-law arrived, I handed them each a note:

> *Often when my mom visited and discovered that I*
> *was going shopping soon with the two of you, she gave*

me a note with some cash in it. She always said, "I am so glad you have those two." Me too! And, so, in memory of my mom, as a way to celebrate her, I now give you the same gift she gave me. How grateful I am for you! Love, Afton

Something—outlet shopping—that had been a sore spot with my mom, now took on a different hue—a celebratory one.

Can We Celebrate Regularly?

We started our tradition in our post-college days.

Over birthday dinners out twice a year, we three friends celebrated the year past, looked ahead to another year of adventure, and talked about boys, new apartments, finding jobs that fit our personalities and gifts, and seeking God through it all.

In years measured now by monthly (or more) dinners out, we three friends have all grown in different ways. Two of us now have husbands, one with adult children and one with teenage children. One of us remains single and wears proudly her titles of Professor and Aunt to twenty-two nieces and nephews.

The year my mom died and the year Michelle's dad died, we kept our birthday dinner tradition. We brought little gifts, asked for lots of cream with our coffee, and laughed and cried together about all that we had lived through that year and how we had struggled to seek God in all of it. We wondered aloud what we would talk about over birthday dinners the next year.

In my year of loss, I so needed those birthday dinners—a time to celebrate friendships that had already endured through so many years and so many life changes and stresses. Friendships that promised more dinners, more birthday cards, more little gifts, more fighting over the cream for coffee, and more challenges to look for God's hand in each day.

One of the cards I cherish from those dinners contains these handwritten words, "Continue to follow your dream, my wonderful friend. You have so much to give. I can't wait to see what God has planned for you this year. Happy Birthday!"

Regular, consistent celebration pulls us back to remembering God's goodness—something God urged His people to do long ago when He initiated the Passover celebration:

"This will be a memorial day for you; you will celebrate it as a festival to God down through the generations, a fixed festival celebration to be observed always" (Exodus 12:14, *The Message*).

What If?

Maybe your friend recently received a promotion at work, an engagement ring, or good news of a child succeeding at something. What do you think might happen inside your heart if you intentionally organized a "rejoicing with you party" for this friend?

Chapter 13

Making Room for Growth

"Do you see any red flags?" I asked the counselor several months after Mom's death. "I want to make sure I'm handling all of this in a healthy way."

"I'm not seeing any at the moment," she responded. I felt elated, almost as if I had gotten an *A* on my report card for a challenging class.

Two years later, however, I once again found myself in a counselor's office. This time I couldn't stop my flow of tears long enough to ask any questions.

Getting out of bed every day had become harder and harder. I had begun to spend more and more time in a dark basement with a blanket over my head. My legs felt so heavy.

My head hurt. Talking and connecting with people took so much energy. Why wouldn't the phone just stop ringing?

Michelle called often during these dark days, but I usually didn't answer the phone. She began to hang up and then call again in a few minutes. And again if necessary. By the third call I usually answered the phone. And then she pushed me gently with some questions, "What is going on? How are you feeling? Do you need to go talk to someone? Remember, Aftonian, 'Because of the Lord's great love we are not consumed, for his compassions never fail. They are new every morning. . . .'" (Lamentations 3:22-23, NIV).

"I'm trying to believe that. I really am. I'm just so sad. Life has piled up on me."

I blamed my kids; I blamed my husband; I blamed God. I felt as if I lived in a dark, dark tunnel. What was it? Another layer of grief? Family stress? Hormonal issues?

Finally, late the afternoon of our wedding anniversary after I had spent the day crying in the basement and refusing to go out to a celebratory dinner, I picked up the phone and called a counselor.

And on that day I began a journey I did not want to take with a companion I would never have chosen: *depression*.

Facing Depression

Part of my journey with depression meant forcing myself to connect with people.

"Let's do a journaling class together for the women at the college. I can't do it by myself. Could you help me?"

On one of my afternoon visits to my friend Helen deVette, she hatched this idea. She knew that I loved words and that I loved learning from her. And, perhaps she also knew that I needed to get out of my house and do something for other women.

She suggested we start with a book by Luci Shaw titled *Life Path: Personal and Spiritual Growth through Journal Writing.* We arranged to meet at my house once a month and to keep each other accountable to journal. Helen gave us assignments. We wrote about life, family memories, God's blessings. . . .

In my journal I learned again to open my soul to God and to myself. These pages became a private, life-giving oasis for me. They pulled me back to words again, where I once again discovered their healing power. Something I would not have discovered without the push of my friend, Helen deVette.

Some days I did not feel like writing.

Some days I did not feel like cleaning my house to host a group of women.

But I had made a promise to my friend. . . .

In her book *Journal Keeping: Writing for Spiritual Growth* (page 60), Luann Budd sums up the effect of journaling so well: "Writing honestly about what is going on inside me is the first step toward living authentically. . . . Renew your resolve to write candidly, to bang on the table, to be honest with yourself."[1]

Through journaling, I have experienced the truth of Psalm 139:23-24: "Search me, O God, and know my heart; test me and know my anxious thoughts. Point out anything in me that offends you, and lead me along the path of everlasting life" (NLT).

Another part of my journey with depression involved returning to things I loved to do, such as writing.

After Mom died, I found great comfort in reading and writing about Leadville, Colorado, specifically the building of an ice palace there in 1896. As I worked, I remembered the Leadville trips we had taken together. And I covered my desk with the books about Leadville Mom had bought for me.

---

1   Luann Budd, *Journal Keeping: Writing for Spiritual Growth,* (Downers Grove, IL: InterVarsity Press, 2002), p. 60.

When my children's book, *Palace of Ice*, came out in 2008, I so wished that Mom could have stood by my side at a book signing, especially the one in my hometown.

That day, also the day of the annual Beer Fest, I fought through crowds of celebrating people to get to the bookstore. Needless to say the crowd inside was small. My childhood friend and her daughter. Our family attorney. And two friends of Mom's. I don't know how any of them found parking that day.

One of Mom's friends told me a story of a writer who tried lots of types of writing as she worked to discover her niche. "Keep writing," she encouraged me. "You will find your niche."

If you haven't already done so, take some time today to begin a journal. Consider beginning by answering some of the questions provided at the back of this book. Ask God to use this practice to open the eyes of your heart.

When the idea for this book first began to take shape, I emailed a few of my mother's friends. They all emailed back and cheered me on:

I think your idea to make this into a book is great. You are such an author now—I am mightily impressed.

*Let's be sure to keep in touch with each other—you
are such a great young woman, and it is an honor to
have younger friends. One that I truly cherish.
—Love to you and yours. J.*

These words reminded me of Paul's words of encouragement and challenge to young Timothy: "For this reason I remind you to fan into flame the gift of God, which is in you through the laying on of my hands. For the Spirit God gave us does not make us timid, but gives us power, love and self-discipline" (2 Timothy 1:6-7, NIV).

Pressing on—Together

Depression, I believe, will always chase me. I have vowed to roll up my sleeves and dig in to fight it with exercise, diet, medication, a balance of work and play, and, maybe especially, consistent walks with my neighbor—my Storm Sister.

I'm not sure exactly when these text messages started, but now they fly every weekday across the street to and from my neighbor's house.

"Walk at 8:15?"

"Yes!"

Our furry boys start to jump and whine when they hear the whoosh of the text coming in. Once outside they greet each other with a high five, while standing on their back legs. Then they ignore each other and begin their peeing contest.

As the boys meander and pee, often barely avoiding each other's heads, my neighbor and I talk. Sometimes we bemoan the weather. Sometimes we laugh at our dogs, especially her dog. (Who wouldn't laugh at a dog who has the face of a Labrador, the body of a Dachshund, and the personality of Beagle?) Some mornings our conversation turns to what weighs on our hearts—work issues, family issues, health issues. . . .

We have done this long enough that we can speak encouragement that rings true: "Parenting is such a challenge isn't it? I'm with you. We're all muddling through. I will pray for you." We can speak honestly with each other and offer words of challenge: "Why are you doing that? Do you think you should say something?"

During times of personal struggle, these morning texts speak hope to me. They challenge me to fight my knee-jerk reaction of pulling into myself and isolating when life gets dark.

My little dog has pulled me into a relationship with my neighbor that has opened my eyes to the truth of Proverbs 27:10: "As iron sharpens iron, so a friend sharpens a friend" (NLT). I wonder if he has any notion of his own wisdom?!

Iron-sharpening-iron friendships. Way back in college I came to know their strength.

We all lived together, first in a dorm and then in an apartment our senior year where we cooked together, cleaned together, laughed together, and challenged each other to grow in our faith in God. We called ourselves the BCM—*Bella Casa Mia*—my beautiful home.

We now live in a variety of states with our husbands. Some of us have a newly empty nest. One of us has recently gone back to work after being home for fifteen years. One of us wears the title of pastor's wife. We all still cook with enthusiasm. Some of us admit to having a passion for coffee at any hour of the day. We all still deeply love God and rely on the Bible for life direction.

Some years ago after a college reunion, we began a regular email. We agreed that these emails would be a safe place to speak honestly. And honest we are. All of us. We write of hopes, worries, struggles, joys, confusion, new insights into life and faith in God. . . . We often ask each other for advice about a sticky situation, and we often ask each other to pray for specific situations. We rejoice with each other as we see God answer prayer: "Amen! Amen! To our God and Father, be glory forever and ever, AMEN! We'll keep praying. Love, L"

How might you build into your schedule a daily (or weekly) connection with a friend?

Above all else we challenge each other to look beyond this world to the next, echoing the words of Paul: "I press on toward the goal to win the prize for which God has called me heavenward in Christ Jesus" (Philippians 3:14, NIV).

Now, instead of crawling into myself when storms hit, I head to my computer and send out an email to my "girls." As one of them said so eloquently, "What a blessing this life of interdependence is!"

What If?

We all struggle with dark times in life. What would you do if you had a friend you suspected suffered from depression?

Chapter 14

Focusing on What We Cannot See

I love happy endings.

As I sat with my mother and watched her slowly fade away, I so wanted to skip over that stress and sorrow and pick up the "Go directly to Joy" card in the board game of life. At other moments in my life I railed against God because He did not come through for me with the happy ending I thought He owed me. And, truthfully, at other moments I caved to despair and muttered to myself, "Life is just grim. Deal with it. Forget about finding joy."

Before she died, my friend Helen deVette gave me a great gift—some of her teaching files. In them I discovered a paper she had written about happy endings in children's literature and a concept J.R.R. Tolkien wrote about in an essay titled "On Fairy Tales." He called this concept "evangelium," a gleam of hope, of joy, that gives us a window into a world beyond this world—heaven.

Perhaps I love happy endings because I have been created for one. Heaven.

I can't write myself into this happy ending. And I can't use my words to fully explain it. And yet I can't deny the tug of my heart toward a reality far beyond this present world. Am I just a hopeless optimist? Or have I too had a glimpse of "evangelium"?

> *Death swallowed by triumphant Life!*
> *Who got the last word, oh, Death?*
> *Oh, Death, who's afraid of you now?*
> *It was sin that made death so frightening and law-code guilt that gave sin its leverage, its destructive power. But now in a single victorious stroke of Life, all three—sin, guilt, death—are gone, the gift of our Master, Jesus Christ. Thank God!*
> —1 Corinthians 15:55-57, The Message

Michelle, more than anyone I know, has one foot here and one foot planted firmly in heaven. Almost as if she can taste heaven. My vision of life beyond this life can easily become clouded with the details of daily living. I remain grateful for Michelle's vision, a vision so clearly described in 2 Corinthians 5:1-8:

> . . . *We know that when these bodies of ours are taken down like tents and folded away, they will be replaced by resurrection bodies in heaven—God-made, not handmade—and we'll never have to relocate our "tents" again. Sometimes we can hardly wait to move—and so we cry out in frustration. Compared to what's coming, living conditions around here seem like a stopover in an unfurnished shack, and we're tired of it! We've been given a glimpse of the real thing, our true home, our resurrection bodies! The Spirit of God whets our appetite by giving us a taste of what's ahead. He puts a little of heaven in our hearts so that we'll never settle for less.*
>
> *That's why we live with such good cheer. You won't see us drooping our heads or dragging our feet! Cramped conditions here don't get us down. They only remind us of the spacious living conditions ahead. It's what we trust in but don't yet see that keeps us going.*

Do you suppose a few ruts in the road or rocks in the path are going to stop us? When the time comes, we'll be plenty ready to exchange exile for homecoming.

The Message

"Aftonian," Michelle reminds me frequently, "remember that this world is not our home. We will always be homesick for home in this world until we reach our true and final home in heaven."

When Darkness Turns to Light

On gloomy, dark days I often think of how my mom's world became increasingly dark during her last months as her disease destroyed the neurons in her brain that enabled her to see. Some days she could laugh about it: "There go my neurons. They're doing their thing again." Other days she seemed overwhelmed with darkness and the destruction going on in her head and wept.

On one of these weepy days, I remember picking up her Bible and reading to her from Psalm 139—one of her favorite Psalms. She quieted visibly as I read. The sound and rhythm of these familiar words seemed to reach inside her troubled brain.

I read: "Where can I go from your Spirit? . . . If I say, 'Surely the darkness will hide me and the light become night around me,' even the darkness will not be dark to you; the night will shine like the day, for darkness is as light to you" (Psalm 139:7,11-12, NIV).

Darkness. And light.

I wondered then if Mom in her brain-altered state would comprehend these verses so full of metaphor? Would they bring her comfort? Would they tell her what I so wanted her to know: "God is here with you. Even though your disease makes everything seem so dark, God is here bringing the light of His peace. And soon, Mom, soon, you will know the everlasting light of heaven—the very real world beyond this dark one."

How does the reality of heaven filter into your daily life and conversations?

When I paused after reading those verses, Mom smiled at me and said, "Those would be good verses for me to remember, wouldn't they?"

"Yes, Mom," I smiled as I wiped tears from my eyes. "Oh, yes, Mom!"

We can't see heaven. We can't see God. Does that mean they don't exist and that we must resign ourselves to living in never-ending darkness? No! Absolutely no!

> . . . *Though outwardly we are wasting away, yet inwardly we are being renewed day by day. For our light and momentary troubles are achieving for us an eternal glory that far outweighs them all. So we fix our eyes not on what is seen, but on what is unseen, since what is seen is temporary, but what is unseen is eternal* (2 Corinthians 4:16-18, NIV).

Many years after Mom died, I discovered these words, written in her almost illegible cursive, reminding me once again of what she could not see but held dear—God.

> *The tree in front of my window shakes itself as if it were freezing, as if the cold evening wind seizes it. . . . And underneath in the street fall leaves on one another—and lose themselves in the night.*
>
> *Now one really says, "The day is dying" because one doesn't see the light anymore.*

And one can think that it moves on farther. But it only goes farther, a little bit farther, climbs up new mountains, shines on new forests and oceans.

It was for a few hours my companion, but now it goes on farther, and I can no longer see it.

When sometime, whether early or late, whether expected or unhoped for, my life, as the day, comes to an end—then the hands of the clock will cut out the end of my time, no matter how things are with me.

Whether I draw my last breath in white pillows, or somewhere in dust and blood on the edge of the street, I don't know how it will be; I only know that sometime the farewell will come, whether dirty or elegant.

Then one says, "Well, now it is over" because I say no further word. You'll go quietly home and think only on the day on which I go farther, only a little farther. I go into God's joy, go into God's light.

I was for a few years your companion, and now I go farther, in order to be with my Lord.

Let us choose light. Let us choose God and accept His gift of eternal life.

When Heaven Appears

For a fleeting moment, I saw heaven.

Mom had not eaten anything for a week. She now lay in bed, sleeping for great portions of every day and night. I had not heard her speak any words for over a week. When a friend came to visit, sometimes her eyes flew open with a hint of recognition. Her friends continued to come. One came and sang hymns to her for a few hours. Others came and sat quietly. When I sat with her, I often played a CD of instrumental hymns.

When I returned to the care facility from a dinner break one evening, I noticed that Mom's breathing had turned raspy, very labored. I realized that the time had come for me to usher Mom to the gates of heaven. Not something I ever imagined I would do. And not something I ever felt prepared to do.

I turned on the CD of hymns and gently took Mom's hand. As the CD began to play one of my favorite hymns, "Thine Is the Glory," I bent down to kiss Mom on the forehead and said, "Mom, I know you love me. I love you too. Jesus is waiting now. Jesus is waiting. You can go to Jesus."

A beautiful smile covered her face, a face that had

become frozen in a look of blankness for the past few days. And then, very softly, she began to hum. Her entire face gradually lit up with an expression of utter joy as her eyes flew open one last time.

And then, she took one last, raspy breath and stepped out of this world and into the next.

"Welcome to heaven," I whispered as I kissed her one last time.

For our dying bodies must be transformed into bodies that will never die; our mortal bodies must be transformed into immortal bodies. Then, when our dying bodies have been transformed into bodies that will never die, this Scripture will be fulfilled: "Death is swallowed up in victory. O death, where is your victory? O death, where is your sting?" (1 Corinthians 15:53-55, NLT).

What If?

At some point we must all face death—our own as well as the death of those we love. If today were your last day on this earth, how would the unseen reality of heaven speak to you?

Study Guide

Your Journey to Storm Sisterhood

Find a quiet spot and a journal and use the questions and statements below to guide your thoughts about your friendships with other women. Push yourself to write and reflect with honesty. Then move on to the questions from the Learning from the Bible section. I believe the Bible speaks truth into our lives and relationships in ways far deeper than our human understanding. Finally, consider working through this study guide with a friend.

Chapter 1
Ingredients for Everyday Friendship

1. What does your daily schedule reveal about how much you value friendship?

2. Do you long for a true friend, a Storm Sister? If so, what changes might you begin to make?

3. Make a list, a short list, of two or three women with whom you would like to nurture a friendship.

4. How will faith in God and study of the Bible, shape the time you spend with these women?

Learning from the Bible

1. What do the following verses tell you about God and His desire to connect with Adam and Eve?

When the cool evening breezes were blowing, the man and his wife heard the Lord God walking about in the garden. So they hid from the Lord God among the trees. Then the Lord God called to the man, "Where are you?" (Genesis 3:8-9, NLT).

2. What does the following verse tell you about the relationship between God and Moses?

Inside the Tent of Meeting, the Lord would speak to Moses face to face, as one speaks to a friend. Afterward Moses would return to the camp, but the young man who assisted him, Joshua son of Nun, would remain behind in the Tent of Meeting (Exodus 33:11, NLT).

3. In the verse below, King Jehoshaphat of Judah references God's friendship with Abraham. How does this reference of friendship between God and a human being speak to you about God's view of friendship?

O our God, did you not drive out those who lived in this land when your people Israel arrived? And did you not give this land forever to the descendants of your friend Abraham? (2 Chronicles 20:7, NLT).

4. Finally, take some time to savor the words below.

But God showed his great love for us by sending Christ to die for us while we were still sinners. And since we have been made right in God's sight by the blood of Christ, he will certainly save us from God's condemnation. For since our friendship with God was restored by the death of his Son while we were still his enemies, we will certainly be saved through the life of his Son. So now we can rejoice in our wonderful new relationship with God because our Lord Jesus Christ has made us friends of God (Romans 5:8-11, NLT).

5. How does knowing that God values friendship with you influence your thinking about your own friendships?

Chapter 2
When the Storms Come

1. As you grew into an adult, how did your focus on friend-ships with women change?

2. What role do women friends play in your life today?

3. How does faith in God factor into your friendships with other women?

Learning from the Bible

1. Read Mark 4:35-41.

2. Describe the storm outside the boat.

3. How did the disciples react to the storm? And Jesus? To what do you attribute their different reactions?

4. The disciples went together to wake Jesus and ask for his help. How might this principle translate into your life during stormy periods?

5. Even the disciples, who knew Jesus well, felt terrified when they saw the power Jesus had over nature. How do you react to this fact, especially in light of your own storms?

Chapter 3
Asking for Help

1. Describe the last time you asked a friend for help.

2. Describe the last time you answered a friend's request for help.

3. Which situation was easier for you? Why?

4. Write your response to this statement: "When I talk to people about hard things in my life, I feel like I am letting God down by not being a strong believer in Him and His power."

Learning from the Bible

1. Read 2 Chronicles 20:1-22. In the reading, what storm did King Jehoshaphat face? And what was his first reaction to that difficult situation?

2. Why do you think Jehoshaphat gathered the people of Judah together to pray instead of just praying to God by himself?

3. Because Jehoshaphat chose to make his need public, how did he benefit? And how did his people benefit?

4. Copy the following verse and put it where you will see it every day—a bathroom mirror, computer screen. . . . You might want to capitalize the word "we." Consider sharing this verse with a friend this week.

For WE have no power to face this vast army that is attacking us. WE do not know what to do, but our eyes are upon you (2 Chronicles 20:12, NIV).

Chapter 4
Resisting the Urge to Fix

1. Which definition describes you best?

____ I am Ms. Mega Fixit. (I am eager to jump in with
my expertise.)

____ I am Ms. Occasional Fixit. (I only offer my expertise
in limited situations and to specific people.)

____ I am Ms. Forget-about-Me-Fixing-Anything. (I never offer my insight or wisdom to others because I'm
sure I have nothing really helpful to say.)

2. Which Ms. Fixit do you wish you really could be? Why?

3. We have all said and done hurtful things in our attempts to help ("fix") other people. Write briefly about one such situation in your life. Then spend some time in prayer giving the situation to God.

4. Think about the friendships in your life today. Which one in particular challenges you because your friend struggles with something? Spend some time thinking and praying about this friendship. Do you consistently try to fix? Do you spend time talking to God about this relationship, asking Him to help you listen with His ears and see with His eyes?

Learning from the Bible

1. Read Jonah 1:11-17.

2. What dilemma did these sailors face because Jonah failed to obey God?

3. Instead of following Jonah's advice, what did the sailors do? And what do you think motivated them?

4. If you had been on the boat with Jonah, what would you have done?

5. What happened when the sailors stopped trying to fix the situation?

6. Do you have a Jonah-type situation in your life? Do you feel as if you work and work to fix situations someone else creates? What might happen if you let go and trusted God to step in and do His work?

Chapter 5
Weeping with Those Who Weep

1. How do you react when other people cry in your presence?

2. Have you ever felt "stuck" in tears? What helped you move beyond those tears?

3. How do you view the hope of heaven, especially as a way to comfort those in sorrow?

Learning from the Bible

1. Read John 11:32-44.

2. How did Jesus react to Mary's accusation that He had come too late to save Lazarus?

3. What moved Jesus to tears?

4. How did Jesus offer hope beyond tears?

5. Jesus literally raised Lazarus from the dead, resurrected him. Just before he did this, He said this to Martha, "I am the resurrection and the life. He who believes in me will live, even though he dies; and whoever lives and believes in me will never die. Do you believe this? " If you were Martha, how would you have answered Jesus?

Chapter 6
Helping in Tangible Ways

1. How would you respond to a friend who said, "Today while you sit at the hospital with your mother-in-law, I would like to do your laundry"?

2. How would you respond if this same friend sent you a gift?

3. How does "doing something" to help another person in distress build your faith in God who did so much for us?

4. And how might doing something tangible to help a hurting friend speak God's love to that person?

Learning from the Bible

1. Read 2 Kings 4:8-10.

2. What did the Shunammite woman do for Elisha?

3. Apparently the Shunammite woman was well-to-do. Based on this brief passage, how does she appear to use her money and possessions?

4. What appears to be her (and her husband's) motivation for doing these things?

5. Elisha found a place of rest and renewal at this home in Shunem. Think about the physical possessions you enjoy—a spa-like bathroom, a backyard oasis, a reliable car, a timeshare, frequent flyer miles. How might you help a storm-tossed friend in a tangible way by sharing some of your possessions?

Read more about this woman and her friendship with Elisha in 2 Kings 4:11-37.

Chapter 7
Respecting Limits

1. Which of the following statements describes you best?

____ I have learned to establish mental boundaries before I agree to help others.

____ Limits? Boundaries? I just jump in and clean up the mess later.

____ I avoid needing to know my limits by avoiding helping people or asking them to help me.

2. What physical and spiritual indicators in your life remind you that you have overstepped your limits?

3. What do you do when you recognize these warning signals? Or, how can you help yourself recognize and respond to these warning signals?

4. Perhaps you have one particular relationship that needs some specific attention. Do you need to change the way you have set limits? What can you do this week? What can you do over the long haul?

Learning from the Bible

1. Read Luke 15:11-31.

2. Why do you think the father in this story said "Yes" when his youngest son asked for his inheritance?

3. What might have happened to the youngest son if the father had said "No"?

4. Why do you think the youngest son asked something of his father that pushed the limits of the cultural practices of that day?

5. What happened to the youngest son when he came to the end of himself, and admitted his limits?

6. Take a moment and think about how God has used limits in your life. How have you responded?

Chapter 8
Offering and Accepting Wise Counsel

1. Describe a time when you gave someone bad counsel. Why did you do it? What did you learn from the situation?

2. Who are the go-to, wise-counsel women in your life? If you do not have such women in your life, who would you like them to be? How might you foster such a relationship?

3. Is God nudging you to speak a word of wise counsel to a friend? How do you distinguish between God's nudge and your own jealousy or anger? How do you discern that you do indeed have wise counsel to offer? Feeling hesitant to speak counsel into a friend's life? Why?

Learning from the Bible

1. Read 2 Samuel 12:1-13.

2. Why did Nathan speak truth to David?

3. Nathan chose to start his hard conversation with David by telling a story. What was the value of doing this?

4. Nathan does not end his story simply by saying, "the end," rather he states boldly, "You are the man!" and goes on to tell David explicitly of his sin. How would you respond if God called you to be a Nathan in a conversation like this one? How would you respond if you were David in such a scenario?

5. How can you prepare your heart so that God might use you to speak wise counsel into the life of a friend? And how can you prepare your heart so that you can truly hear wise counsel from the lips of a friend?

Chapter 9
Sharing Important Events

1. Make a list of the top four best events in your life. Who shared these events with you? How did that make a difference to you?

2. Now make a list of the top four worst events in your life. Who shared these events with you? How did that make a difference to you?

3. Spend some time now writing a prayer to God asking Him to open your heart to sharing important—good and not-so-good—events with a specific friend.

Learning from the Bible

1. Read Job 32:11-13.

2. When Job's three friends heard about all the hard things that had happened to him, why did they go to visit him?

3. What did the three friends do when they saw Job? And then why do you think they said nothing for seven days?

4. How do you react when you hear about something hard happening in the life of a friend? Why do you react this way?

5. How might you react to someone being present with you in your grief but saying nothing? Would you feel comfortable doing this for a friend? Why or why not?

You can read more about Job's friends, who did not remain silent, in Chapters 4, 5 8, and 11. Don't miss God's response to their words in Chapter 38.

Chapter 10
Making Time to Listen

1. Picture yourself in a setting either with one friend or with a group of friends. How would you describe your listening abilities in such a setting?

____ I am happy to sit and let the conversation swirl around me.

____ Honestly, I tune out most of the conversation and keep thinking about what I want to say next.

____ Sitting in silence bothers me so I usually speak my mind to fill the silence.

2. How might your listening tendencies hurt or help a friend going through a storm?

3. If you asked a close friend to describe your listening abilities, what would she say? (Consider asking her if you feel brave!)

4. What practical steps could you implement in your friendships to become a friend who offers the gift of listening? Hosting a get-together in which you ask each guest to answer a question? Starting a group email with three or four like-minded friends?

Learning from the Bible

1. Read Nehemiah 5:1-13.

2. What did the people complain about?

3. Although Nehemiah focused on rebuilding the wall around Jerusalem, what did he do when he heard these complaints?

4. Listening to the poor in Jerusalem no doubt delayed Nehemiah's building project. Why do you think he did it?

5. What do you suppose would happen in our day if leaders listened more and talked less?

6. What can you learn from Nehemiah's life that could affect your friendships, especially during stormy times?

Chapter 11
Reaching across Generations

1. What have you learned from people older (or younger) than you?

2. At this stage in your life, what generational connections do you have? If you do not have any, what keeps you from making such a connection?

3. Given a full schedule of your own, how can you realistically make time to invest in someone of another generation?

4. How has God worked in your life and how might hearing about that journey help someone of a younger (or older) generation?

Learning from the Bible

1. Read Ruth 1:1-18.

2. How did these three widows of different generations plan together to cope with their loss of their husbands and their need for food?

3. Both younger women, Orpah and Ruth, initially refused to abandon Naomi on her journey back to Jerusalem. But then Orpah did turn around and go home to her mother. What likely changed her mind? (Consider Naomi's speech in verses 11-13.)

4. Ruth opted to stay with her mother-in-law despite the fact that the journey would be rough and Naomi had nothing to offer her, especially another husband. What might have motivated Ruth?

5. These two women of different generations willingly wove their lives together, and as a result they both experienced great joy. Don't miss the end of the story in Ruth 4:13-17. Is God nudging you to invest in a trans-generational relationship? Don't turn back and miss the joy ahead.

Chapter 12
Rejoicing with Those Who Rejoice

1. How does faith in God figure into your ability to rejoice with others? Does it give you strength or cause guilt? Why?

2. What do you perceive to be the value in celebrations—times of rejoicing with each other?

3. How might you welcome God into your celebrations with friends?

Learning from the Bible

1. Read Philippians 2:17-18 and 3:1.

2. How does Paul acknowledge his own feelings and situation even as he talks about rejoicing?

3. What do you think helped Paul not to fixate on the dismal circumstances of his life and find the strength and perspective and will to rejoice with the Philippians?

4. In Philippians 3:1, what does Paul mean when he urges, "Rejoice in the Lord!"? How might you do this? And how might this affect your ability to "rejoice with those who rejoice"?

5. When you struggle in a dark situation as Paul was, and people around you appear to thrive, do you tend toward self-pity or toward "rejoicing with those who rejoice"? Why?

6. How do Paul's words and example challenge you as you think about the way you respond to grief and hard times in your life?

Chapter 13
Making Room for Growth

1. What do you fear in developing a friendship that involves accountability and challenge?

2. Think back to a time when you wanted to challenge a friend but decided not to do so. What happened to your friendship?

3. Are you able and willing to invest time in becoming a Storm Sister? What holds you back? How might you make a start, even just one small step?

Learning from the Bible

1. Read Exodus 4:10-16.

2. God called Moses to speak words of challenge to Pharaoh. How did Moses respond?

3. And how did God counter Moses' response?

4. When have you, like Moses, said, "Please send someone else to do it"? Why?

5. How did God help Moses face his fear? And how might God help you face your fear of becoming a Storm Sister who can speak words of challenge?

6. Spend some time in prayer, asking God to give you courage as you commit yourself to becoming a Storm Sister, one who does not fear to hear or to speak words of challenge and encouragement.

Chapter 14
Focusing on What We Cannot See

1. Lots of people today talk and write about heaven. Why do you think they do it?

2. How easily do you put your trust in what you cannot see? Why?

3. Life moves at a busy pace, so full of important details. Why should anyone take the time to contemplate what lies beyond this world, beyond death of our human bodies?

Learning from the Bible

1. Read Mark 2:1-5.

2. The paralytic man needed help from others. He knew it. Although likely not crippled, what traits do we share with this man?

3. What huge gesture of friendship did this paralytic man receive?

4. What would you do if you had a paralyzed friend, and you knew someone who had a cure?

5. We live in a world—neighborhoods, families, friendships—people crippled by sin who do not know that Jesus can heal and offer the joy of new life on this earth and an eternity beyond description. What can you say to these paralyzed people? How will you live among them as a Storm Sister? Storm Sisterhood has no other higher purpose.

Thine is the glory,
Risen, conqu'ring Son;
Endless is the vict'ry
Thou o'er death hast won.

Words from Cantate Domino by permission of the World Student
Christian Federation, Geneva.

Source: "Thine Is the Glory, Risen, Conquering Son," Hymns for the Living
Church, (Carol Stream, IL: Hope Publishing Company, 1984), p. 171.

Notes

Notes

Notes

Notes

Notes

Notes

Suggested Books for Storm Sisters

Brestin, Dee. *Friendships of Woman: The Beauty and Power of God's Plan for Us.* Colorado Springs: David C. Cook; 2nd edition, 2005.

Budd, Luann. *Journal Keeping: Writing for Spiritual Growth.* Downers Grove, IL: InterVarsity Press, 2002.

Packer, J.I. *Knowing God.* Downers Grove, IL: InterVarsity Press, 1993.

Rubietta, Jane. *Quiet Places: A Woman's Guide to Personal Retreat.* Grayslake, IL: Abounding Publishing, 1997.

Shaw, Luci. *Life Path: Personal and Spiritual Growth through Journal Writing.* Vancouver, BC: Regent College Publishing. 2004.

Life Application Study Bible: New Living Translation. Carol Stream, I: Tyndale House Publishers, Inc., 2004.

About the Author

Afton Rorvik enjoys her roles as wife, mother, friend, editor, and writer. She loves shaping words, reading books by contemplative authors, listening to music, drinking coffee with friends, traveling, and savoring the words in her favorite book—the Bible.

She has been a part of the publishing industry since 1987, editing a myriad of adult nonfiction books for the CBA market, while working with both first-time authors and best-selling authors. Her articles have appeared in *Discipleship Journal, Guideposts, NAB Today,* and *Wheaton.* She is a graduate of Wheaton College with a degree in literature as well as a teaching certificate in secondary education. She and her husband John live in Wheaton, Illinois. They are the parents of two adult children.

Visit aftonrorvik.com to read her blog on
friendship and overcoming the storms of life.
You can also follow Afton on Facebook and Twitter.